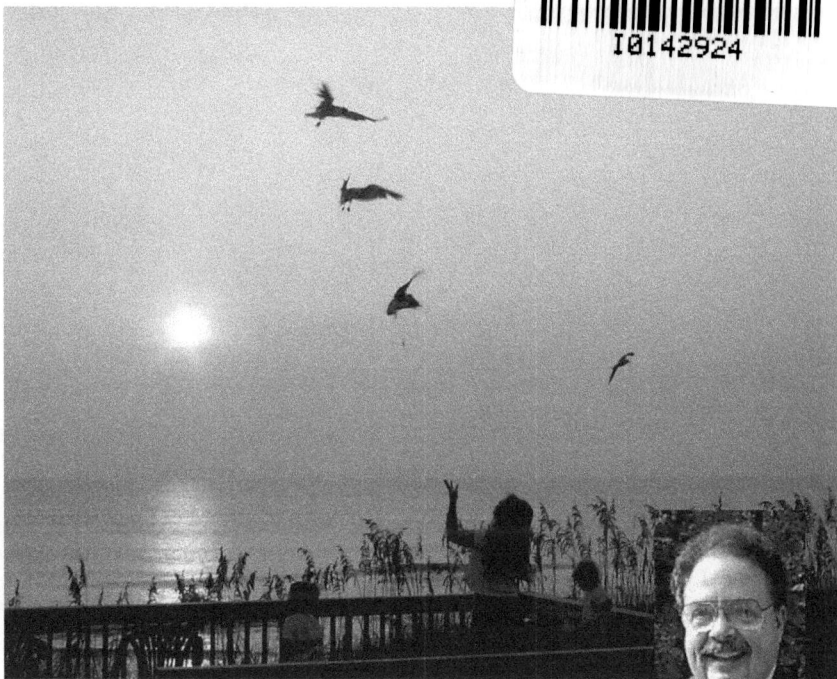

About the Author

C. Page Highfill, AIA Emeritus, is an architect (ret), author, writer, speaker and photographer. His photo above shows family members feeding sea gulls at sunrise at Nags Head, NC. This is the source photo selected to reveal transparency in the fonts of the Twelve Words title. Through such transparency one sees the heart of the messages contained here.

Page's earlier writing and presentations on creative systems generated wide colleague interest with invitations to speak at three National AIA Conventions, and various AIA Chapter Conferences throughout the country. He also served on over a dozen University of Wisconsin seminars for architects and engineers. He was a frequent speaker at the International A/E Systems conferences throughout the USA. His architectural work has been honored by the American Institute of Architects both nationally and state-wide. His first book, Thin Places and Five Clues in Their Architecture was published in 2009.

Page has written magazine articles, poems and essays throughout his career. He has also written and directed over 13 faith-based drama productions for local churches. His article submitted to the Future Ideas of Tomorrow competition, sponsored by the American Institute for Design and Drafting received the first place award. He is a graduate of Virginia Tech and is listed in Who's Who in the South and Southwest.

WHAT OTHERS ARE SAYING…

Page has compiled a collection of written works that explain and illustrate twelve key concepts that will provide the reader with insight on making the most of their journey through life. His poems, essays and short stories focus on specific elements of life, which he has distilled from his experiences, and from these experiences he offers the seeker an opportunity to empathize with his trials, achievements and disappointments, and perhaps come to a fuller appreciation of the diverse rewards and achievements one can attain in their quest for purpose and a meaningful existence. These concepts are summarized in twelve words, which provide a foundation for the development of his gift to the reader, lessons on discovering their maximum potential and a meaningful life."

Dr. Dean L. Collings, Sr.

Twelve Words Never to Forget is an insightful study of important concepts to enrich our lives as we seek meaning and purpose in our life experiences and how to bless others we meet along the way. C. Page Highfill has gathered a lifetime of experiences, lessons, observations and writings, to show us the way to a richer and fuller life. He has some wonderful insights and great ways of putting complicated thoughts into an easy to understand format. Readers will enjoy and learn a lot and indeed be better equipped for a deeper and more successful life. The twelve words are an easy pneumonic device for remembering the lessons so as to more effectively apply them as we continue our life journeys.

Carol McLaren

This is a book you'll perhaps need/want to read more than once. Page Highfill relates 12 key words in life to lessons he has learned over the years. They are interesting questions/observations he raises that drew this reader deeper into his own mind, motivations and self.

Rev. Tom Lacy
Founder/Co-director Richmond Christians Who Write.

WHAT OTHERS ARE SAYING...*(continued)*

Page Highfill, playwright, artist and author, pursued as avocations, a true renaissance man. His earlier book *Thin Places* gives meaning to those déjà vu moments we all experience from time to time; the feeling that where we are is somewhere between where we were and where we'll someday be.

In contrast *Twelve Words* is a collection of stories, poems and song lyrics designed to invoke thoughts from within. Various entries will appeal to a wide range of ages and interest, and everyone will find those that speak to them. The joy of this book is anticipation; it's all about the journey. Just as tomorrow brings expectation... so too does *Twelve Words* ... a story ... that poem which speaks to you might be but a page away.

G. Wesley Childress

TWELVE
WORDS

Never to Forget

By C. Page Highfill, AIA Emeritus
Architect (ret), writer, speaker and granddad

Twelve life-building lessons from a generation of writings to guide you to higher levels of success and meaning.

TWELVE WORDS
Never to Forget

By C. Page Highfill, AIA Emeritus
Architect (ret), writer, speaker and granddad

Twelve life-building lessons from a generation of writings to guide you to higher levels of success and meaning.

EnterPaths, L.L.C., Publisher
http://www.EnterPaths.com/

Orders: http://stores.lulu.com/pagehighfill
Information: http://www.EnterPaths.com/

ISBN:978-0-578-06616-5

This book is dedicated to God,
known by many names, nods and nurtures,
and while I specifically choose one of them,
I dedicate this book to all expressions: the whole;
the universally intrinsic; all ways and histories,
which seek to ennoble for all – glimpses of the Divine.

This book is also dedicated to my late beloved wife, Kate;
my mother, Mary; my father, Henry; and my mother-in-law,
Ada, all of whom now reside in heaven as we continue
to experience their life-influences upon us.

This book is also dedicated to my four children,
Scott, Marc, Ann Page and Katie;
and their spouses Cindi, Sharon, Rob and Bruce; and
their children, Bryan, Holly, Sean, Austin, Matt, Riley,
Davis, Kyle, Jake, Sydney, Brooke, Rebekah, Olivia and Clare.

This book is also dedicated to my brother and two sisters,
Jerry, Pat and Betty Jean; their spouses Shirley, John and Ken;
their children Anne, Leigh, Jerl, David, Mark, and Kevin; their
spouses Phil, Helene, Diane and Amy; and their children John Jerl,
Joseph, Katelyn, Jack, Hannah, Olivia, Sam, John, Lauren and Allie.

This book is also dedicated to Hampden-Sydney College,
Hampden-Sydney, Virginia, and to its leaders, Trustees,
administrative and facility staff, professors
and students, with whom we all worked and shared
treasured opportunities for nearly twenty years
to further her noble mission.

The above dedication order of God, Family and Career was introduced to me in 1965 by the late Helen Fulton, teacher of a new Bible study class for young married couples and named the Doubles Class, at River Road Church, Baptist. It was not until later that I learned the wisdom of this priority in life. In the language of the Twelve Words, this book is dedicated to the reader's highest levels of success and meaning as may be found in that same order. I hope the reader will delight in discovering all of the life-building lessons invested like seeds planted in the Twelve Words garden, now waiting to be harvested.

TWELVE WORDS
Never to Forget

CONTENTS

**independent elements into a complex interrelating whole.
A team. May we be reminded of this important word in
this tenth month of October, when Halloween's
SYSTEMIC rituals and costumes celebrate the haunt.**

11 ELEVENTH WORD **"COINCIDENCE"** 141

**Most are not. And it is no COINCIDENCE that this word
has 11 letters, reminding us to connect this word with the
eleventh month of November.**

12 TWELFTH WORD **"ACCOUNTABLE"** 151

**Being held accountable is often viewed as a punishment,
yet instead, it is a vital opportunity to learn and grow.
Being left consistently un-ACCOUNTABLE may result in
a false reality. May this twelfth word be remembered by
considering the twelfth month as a perfect time to account
for funds before shopping begins.**

APPENDIX   165

Disclaimer – Warning

This book is written to share example life lessons found by the author while nurturing his family and businesses over the years. This book is offered and sold with the understanding that the publisher and author are not engaged in rendering professional family counseling, legal, financial management or other professional services here. If such services or other expert assistance is required, the services of a competent professional should be sought. Readers are encouraged to involve their own families, friends and associated counselors in any specific applications of the information contained herein.

It is not the purpose of this book to reprint all of the information that is otherwise available on this subject, but instead to complement, amplify and supplement other texts. You are urged to read other available material, learn as much as possible about key words for families and tailor the information to your individual and family needs. For more information, see the various web sites available from search engines responding to family services and values search.

Parenting and guiding family members towards maturity is not a simple or quick process. Most parents learn by trial and error while also reading and discussing numerous opinions with family members plus those from qualified competent counselors and family practice professionals. Sharing the information in this book within your professional team is encouraged as an effective way to move forward with some of the benefits you may see contained herein.

Every effort has been made to make this book as complete and as accurate as possible. However, there may be mistakes, both typographical and in content. Therefore, this text should be used as a general guide which should be tailored to suit your own specific needs and family members.

The purpose of this book is to educate, inspire and entertain. The author and the publisher shall have neither liability nor responsibility to any person or entity with respect to any loss or damage caused, or alleged to have been caused directly or indirectly, by the information contained in this book. If you do not agree with the above, you may return this book to the publisher for a full refund.

PREFACE
About These Twelve Words

This book is a collection of sixty stories, song lyrics, poems and pranks through which twelve life building lessons are revealed and summarized to guide and inspire readers to new levels of success and meaning. The collection was written over a lifetime of teachable moments, those times when the human spirit was captured and then delivered a new view of some aspect of truth and meaning. At the times when most of these stories were written, I had no idea of why I felt the need to write them down. But I did. Writers like musicians and other artists, don't consider or need to know why they do what they do; they just do.

Then, while sharing some of them with family and friends, suggestions were made and finally considered to compile them into some type of organized arrangement for the benefit of future generations including my fourteen grandchildren. It was during the compiling and writing process that the structure of life building lessons rose through the more than 45,000 words found here. Eventually each of those lessons revealed its actions, engagements and influences on us through the twelve single-word names and their summaries.

Each of the twelve words then became a chapter heading with the stories organized and supported with new writings to illustrate the heart of each life building lesson.

You will find reflected throughout my writings here, even those I wrote many years ago, the belief that God is everywhere and unchanging. And, it is our <u>perception</u> of God that changes, fades, grows and often vanishes among today's racing pace. Throughout history, humanity has been given paths to help us connect with God. Holy Scripture, prayer, music, art, architecture, beauty, ritual and service for others are important ones. My mission here is to weave such paths into the daily lives of others through these stories, illustrations, writings and poems to help open hearts and spirits to receive the presence of your God – by whatever name you wish to call him or it, and which of course is actually already there, in each of us. Waiting.

The purpose of this book is to inspire and empower readers to look at the preciousness and potentials of their being, alongside twelve lamp posts (life lessons) which shine powerful energy on all of us. Then as readers continue to experience their own lives, it is hoped they will find further illumination from the twelve life lessons. An easy way to remember the twelve is to associate each word name with one of the months of the year. The month order is also the chapter numbers. The chapter order of the Twelve Words is not an order of life's priority, but only the order I wish to unfold them to you. Each word is **BOLD** as follows:

1 – January: **YOU** your life began with you.

2 – February: **SPIRIT** your second nature.

3 – March: **DREAM** as March dreams of spring.

4 – April: **GOD** who brings April showers from heaven.

5 – May: **LOVE** is in this month of Mother's Day.

6 – June: **FAITH** weds relationship with trust.

7 – July: **HUMOR** as in seven clowns at a July cookout.

8 – August: **HEALTH** stays in shape before the school year.

9 – September: **OTHERS** watch out at school crossings.

10 – October: **SYSTEMIC** as in Halloween costumes.

11 – November: **COINCIDENCE** also has eleven letters.

12 – December: **ACCOUNTABILITY** as before shopping.

Now, let's begin. I will meet YOU on the next page.

~ ~ ~

1 - THE FIRST WORD
"YOU"

You are the sum of your individuality,
your preciousness, your soul.

Olga's School Class

Olga, the teacher, received a memo from the Chief to pass on an important message to her students -- in her own words. She studied the memo, and the next day gave an assignment to her students.

"It has come to my attention," she announced, "that one of you in this room possesses a very special hidden power. The person is not aware of such a gift. But, how to use that power is held deep within that person's memory. It is held in a story about one's most inner spirit -- a story that holds the secret key to this person's life."

Olga walked around the room, as if looking for this very special person, glancing down at each student as she walked by. "How could it be?" The students wondered. "Everyone here is just like me."

Olga continued to move through the classroom. "And, while the story can never be told in detail," she said, "others may get a glimpse of the power it speaks by looking closely for this person. For, when someone else looks into this person's face and imagines that this may in fact be the one who holds the magical gift -- and if so -- one will see a warm glowing radiation appear across the person's face. The observer will unquestionably recognize the glow, but it will not be detected if the observer doesn't truly believe that this person could actually be the one."

Olga walked back to her desk and in her usual fashion, took out her worn black and white speckled spiral notebook and began reading from her notes. "Your assignment students," she said, "is to find out who this person is. You are to work on this during recess, when you are moving around with each other anyway. Search to identify this person. There are five simple rules you must follow in this assignment. Listen to these very carefully."

"1) You cannot ask directly, "Are you the one?" Because, the person doesn't actually know if he or she is the one. Only the Chief and I know the answer to this assignment.

2) You will not learn the answer by grouping around one of your classmates, then comparing notes. The glow will only appear to a sincere and direct observation by you personally.

3) When recess ends, everyone will return to the class here. Then, take a piece of paper and write your name at the top, as you always do. Below your name write the name of the person you think holds this magical power -- and whose eyes reveal that truth to you.

4) If, after you have considered your answer carefully, you are still undecided between two or more possible candidates, write each of the names on your paper. Then, sign it and turn it in, face down on my desk as usual.

5) I will read your papers just after the recess bell rings. And, I will comment on your answers at that time."

The assignment went as directed. The students mingled and giggled with their visual confrontations. Soon, the recess bell sounded, the selections were noted and all of the papers were turned in, face down on Olga's desk. She walked into the room. Standing behind her faded wooden desk, she picked up the stack of papers and slowly read each one. Then, she paused and smiled, looking out at her class, glancing at each for a brief moment.

"Your papers are all correct", she said. "But, you are also all incorrect." She leaned forward across her desk top, using her arms to hold her up, so she could gaze out closer to them. Her eyes were now wide with adoration and wonder for each of them. As the students made eye contact with her, a glow came across Olga's face that every student could plainly see.

"Do you see it now?" She asked. "Now, look at each other again. See?"

As they turned their attention to each other, in wonder, then back to Olga, she whispered to them, "This is the complete answer to the assignment," she said softly, as she raised her right hand from the desk, holding her class role listing every student in the class. "You are the answer. All of you."

~ ~ ~

Your Life Focus Snippet (LFS)

The Olga story introduces us to the importance of seeing the possibilities, potentials and specialness of each individual, the YOU in you and the YOU in others. You have the responsibility in your early teens up through adulthood to be in charge of yourself to discover what makes you tick, and to discover your natural talents and passions. You also need to know your natural shortcomings to help you develop work-arounds to prevent such from holding you back.

Being in charge of yourself also means that you need to start working on building a life focus paragraph description (a snippet) very early in life to help you explore these questions. Where would you like to go in life? What's the best way you can get there? I call this paragraph description Your Life Focus Snippet (LFS) a simple two or three sentence description of yourself, your values, possible fields of interest, and things you can do best to help others. The LFS is the first step in developing an eventual personal mission statement – a more detailed and specific statement of how you envision what you have to offer the world and how that might be best delivered. Both the snippet and the statement are part of a lifetime self examination process which is vitally essential to help you explore and prepare yourself for meaningful life experiences based on the unique YOU. Writing it down is one of the clues to effectiveness. I suggest you write and edit your LFS as often as you have new ideas. Write it as an e-mail to yourself and save it as a draft, even on your cell phone. Refer to it often, change it, add to it, and watch it work for you.

For example, a student LFS might be something as simple as this: *"I'm good in math and I love sports and inspiring people to do their best. Maybe I'll be a high school coach and teach math. Maybe a college coach."* Another one might be: *"There's something about helping young kids that brings me joy. Maybe it's that glow in their eyes when they finally get it."* Simple sentences in your LFS reflecting your perceptions can become valuable building blocks for your later personal mission statement, and most importantly, your life.

If you are a parent, you're the head coach for the first 16 years or so of each of your children in this important examination process. You are an important part of their understanding this YOU process as well as honoring others pursuing their own YOU process. Building a life of joyful service is a complicated process riddled with fears and human needs to belong, to be of worth, and to be competent in career and social choices. Show them how to build their ideas and dreams in their LFS. The best way to do this is to build your own LFS and personal mission statement. One of the joys I experience is watching someone else's LFS or mission statement unfold right before my eyes. Look at what happened to me just the other day.

Recently my wife and I were in a hospital out-patient waiting room. The check-in procedures are usually fairly standard at such places, I thought. Upon entering the room, you stop at a nearby desk or counter and present the attendant with your procedure order; your name is checked off, and you are asked to have a seat. Then you wait to be called to one of the numbered registration desks. After a seemingly unending wait, your name is announced over the ceiling loud speakers to go to desk number 6. This is the standard procedure many of us have experienced over the years.

But this recent waiting room experience revealed a different approach. Instead of the loud speaker announcement, the service person at desk number 6 walked out into the waiting room and almost too quietly announced the first name of who was next. If two or more people looked up, the service person would quietly say the last name. Then, the identified person would get up and go up to the service person who greeted him or her by the first name. Together they walked over to desk number 6.

This struck me as very interesting, not just from the aspect of courtesy. Something special was happening here. Later as we sat down at our registration desk, I complimented the service person with how impressed I was with this reception processing procedure. She immediately responded with, "Yes, this is much better." That confirmed to me that this had been discussed probably many times before by the staff and now had become the intentional well thought-out procedural change – most likely suggested by one of the service people. Bravo to them. It works. I hope whoever came up with the idea received a good bonus. This procedure also appears to me to reflect what we might find by reading one of those framed wall mounted Mission Statements out in the hallway that often include something like, "… to be courteous and friendly to patients…" But in this case, someone carried those mission promises to a practical and creative every day level. Bravo for that too. But there is even more to learn here.

We see here a demonstration of the power of human connectivity and appreciation when the intentions of care and love for others are actually strongly reflected in official operating procedures. This is an early introduction to Word 10 Systemic, whereby a policy becomes alive (systemically) throughout an organization. In this waiting room case it was, and is, a living mission statement. Now, this doesn't happen automatically or easily. First and foremost, it has to be acknowledged that essentially all operating procedures contain human engagement opportunities to demonstrate goodness and intentional concern. It's the same in relationships. The perception of intent is very important. Successful businesses know this, just as successful relationships respect this word intent. It's so vital and elementary that often it is forgotten and excluded. What intentions do you believe are expressed by the loud speakers yelling out one's name among 65 strangers? How about, "we don't care." Or "you're just a number to us." Seems about right doesn't it?

So, what's really happening here? Three important learning points emerged here: First, mission statements which express personal, business, professional and institutional intentions are like seeds to grow what and how we wish to relate and serve. It is a "Pledge of Allegiance" of goals and intentions. Writing them down forces us to reach down (and up) to assemble the highest intentions we can find to form the basis of what we or our business, institution, etc. wish to do. The Bible is a great resource for this too. Start searching through the book of Proverbs. Perhaps select the book of Romans next.

LPSs and mission statements are never "finished." The best ones are works in process, continually being edited and updated as new opportunities present themselves. I suggest you Google "mission statements" and "personal mission statement." At this writing I got 23,900,000 Google hits on "mission statement." Check out the Starbucks mission statement. I got 33,100 Google hits on "personal mission statement," including many on how to build a personal mission statement. The idea is not to simply throw some words down on paper or screen. That will become apparent when you begin to form your own words to explain what you are striving for, what character traits and talents you have to support your choices and which need help. The reason this is difficult is that many of our current choices are selected without much thought or delegated to us by our social culture.

Without a mission statement to shine its clarifying light ahead of the influence of culture to guide your steps and thinking processes, you, like the rest of us, may tend to follow the crowd. You may tend to allow culture to lead the way with its loudspeakers screaming at you to accept being treated like a number. An absent mission statement is a no-plan effort to drift and follow the currents and flighty goals of an all-consuming culture which lives by the phrase, "ready, fire, aim." Sometimes even the aim is left off. It's a no-plan, without meaning or genuine connectivity - which encourages one to fall short of optimizing personal potentials and accomplishing personal goals. There is only one person who can stop that from happening to you. And that person is YOU.

The second point is LFSs and mission statements of goals and relational intentions which are purposely practiced "systemically" will achieve by far the highest levels of goal accomplishment. We will cover Word 10 Systemic in more detail later. Right now I simply wish to connect this Word 1 YOU with Word 10 SYSTEMIC. Hanging a framed mission statement on the wall down the hall is not systemic. Incorporating mission statement intentions into staff meetings and into your personal activities and procedures which engage people is systemic. Someone at that hospital has the right idea on this, because I found that same refreshing caring intention from the technicians down the hall and in the cafeteria. Someone planted that intentional caring seed not only in a few departments, but throughout the hospital, like it circulates in the ductwork throughout the hospital air, mesmerizing employees, patients and visitors to "share the care." What a winner! Do you see the potential here? And to think that this waiting room caring example may have started from a word or two in someone's LFS or mission statement, then on to a staff meeting, and then on to another one, and soon to all of them.

The third point is that intent is a very powerful communicator producing either a negative engagement or a positive one. The Taj Mahal in Agra India is one of the most popular architectural landmarks in the world. It is a tomb building and landscape built by Shah Jehan for his young wife who died almost 400 years ago. The Shah loved his wife so dearly that he built the Taj Mahal to honor her and to show the world how much her love meant to him. I can imagine the Shah communicating this to his architect and insisting that his love for her must be radiated by the entire place, its structures, gardens, reflecting pool and all parts therein. This was his loving intention. Today, the Taj Mahal continues to draw thousands of visitors each year, many motivated to visit from comments made by previous visitors – as they were overcome, many to tears, by the powerful expressions of love radiating from this beautiful composure of forms, spaces and water. It is not just the architecture in itself, but what it conveys – intentions of love.

We all have opportunities to engage people through our intentions and actions of care for others and our love for those beyond ourselves. These are opportunities to be treasured. You may see this happening between a college president engaging with the staff and students, or a business president engaging with the employees, or a dad engaging with his beloved family. You can build and support this powerful engagement process in your life by focusing on your snippet to nudge you along by just a few words of your vision to best share your love in service for others. Then as you tweak, edit and expand your snippet into your personal mission statement, it becomes a refined story-board of what can be, what will be, and what is. This is the wonderful unique YOU, wiggling to become a butterfly here in God's garden of life.

~ ~ ~

Is Life Scripted?

Preface. This is from several e-mails shared between my oldest son and me years ago regarding his question – is life scripted.

Dear son. I believe we have an intended purpose, or script, that our soul knows, and is leaning towards and wishing for, while our physical and intellectual selves continue on in the driving seat. It's like our soul is riding in the back seat, whispering comments and suggestions to us, many of which we don't hear, because we are preoccupied with looking at all of the actions and distractions through the windshield. In many instances, you and I seem to share similarities in our whispers and driving. For example, we are both involved in successful businesses (art and architecture) which we also enjoy, but our "soul whispers" seem to (maybe also) come from another level. Yours from the beauty of various compositions, not only in art and marketing media, but also in your landscaping and plantings (which are pathways to the soul's language) and mine from various compositions of words and art forms (photos, sketches, etc.). My soul longs for ways to explore and express to others the sacred feelings of beauty...as a reflection of God's presence among us. And your soul seems to find a heavenly connection in your landscaping, which is a wonderful canvas on which to paint your whispers. You are doing a wonderful job.

I think my script leads me in a similar direction. While architecture has been an excellent career and training program (service for others) and provider (gasoline) to help me see the lines of the script (whispers) as I drive, now, I feel that it is time for me to shift drivers, as we two (soul and physical driver) are seeing close to the same view out of the windshield. But the soul, with spirited and systemic connections to the Divine, is better equipped to make choices along the way. This is what I call retirement, not to stop driving, but simply to switch drivers.

~ ~ ~

Two Other Drivers

This is a brief parallel story of person walking along the road because he ran out of gas. He was picked up by a passing car. It was a strange situation. The person driving was very calm, and caring. The person on the back seat was an adult but was child-like, playing with toys, making animation sounds for the toys. A brief discussion followed. I learned that the person driving considered himself as the higher self, while the person on the back seat was the ego self. The driver was holding a precious glowing stone which has been a meditative focus of his during much of his life. The ego self used to be driver, but they switched a few miles back.

They finally dropped me off at a gas station. I turned to wave thanks and noticed the license plate on the back of car as it pulled away. It read, "My Body"

~ ~ ~

Bloom, as a Verb

Preface. This is an essay on stress, perhaps too often an unwanted presence in the life of so many of us "You's." This metaphor story offers a fresh look at it from a different perspective. It will test your patience at first, and then reveal the meaning of the title above.

At first, you feel the same as you normally do when you

awaken from a long and comfortable sleep. You twist a little, and extend a minor stretch to regain some of your connections with yourself. You are not yet quite sure where you are or what day it is. You know its December, but you're not yet sure of the day. That's normal, you think. It is a part of your natural awakening fog. You know it will clear soon, and you will be back in reality. But today, somehow, it's different.

You then realize that you are in a new place. It is warm and very sunny, almost too warm. You can feel the heat pouring over your entire body. Somehow, you haven't awakened fully yet. You try. But you cannot see. You can partially sense your surroundings...as if your eyes have been transformed to all parts of your body. You can't see images, but you can sense them through your arms and body.

Now, you noticed the same transformation of your hearing. You must now be fully awake, but your ears apparently aren't. You can feel vibrations of sound all around you. You understand the sounds of your home, like the furnace running again, down in its dark room with dozens of cardboard storage boxes, among collections of memories and dust. It's running again to supply heat to the rest of the house. But you can't really hear it now. You just feel and understand the sound. What's happening here?

As you try and gather your wits, you realize you are standing up, in your living room, in full sunlight next to one of the large windows facing the sun. The warmth covers your body, and you feel especially magnetized by the bright energy.

You stand as if you are some type of transformed antenna positioned before the sun, waiting for new signals to be sent and received. Later, the day begins to end. You can't determine the exact time, especially in your new state. But you can feel the daylight diminishing. The radiating heat drops off substantially. Still, you can't move. Your feet are firmly planted in a fixed position. You must continue to stand.

Then, night time begins to fall. You feel a chill coming from the window just next to you. You try and step back, away from the cold, but your feet won't move. You can feel your toes, like you're standing on the beach after a storm, wiggling in the moist sand. But you can't move your legs. Your body is apparently committed to this position. The chill gets worse. Your finger tips begin to stiffen with the cold. As they get colder...it is as if they begin sending messages to your body. First, there are messages of stress and the pain of bitter cold so close to the window here. You can feel the messages travelling from your fingertips down your arms to your body and to your brain. Then, the messages seem to reverse directions. Now there are reply messages being sent back from the brain, through the body back to your fingertips. Apparently they are new directions to counter the cold, or somehow use the darkness and cold for a next step here. You can feel the messages flow, and you feel a slight burning sensation in your arms and then fingers...as if to warm the passageways in preparation for new body substances and chemicals to arrive at the scene, at your cold and numb fingertips.

You drift off to a standing sleep, wincing with stress and this bad experience. Why is this happening to you?

Soon, it's morning. Then it's the sun again. Fingertips are still swollen, but warm. You continue reaching for the sunlight, and the swelling gets worse and so does the pain.

It's night time again; then day; then, night again. You're growing weaker. Your body has gone into some type of temporary hibernation, except the fingernails. They get heavy, very heavy as if they have grown to be nearly as long as your fingers. The weight signals new strength to your hands and arms. You hold them up. You feel a sense of accomplishment as your hands are drawn hard to the sunlight, even stronger than before. You feel your fingernails begin to unfold into three, four and five new fingernails, like umbrellas catching all they can.

You can feel the sun's warmth, carrying new nourishment you have never felt before. Your whole body aims itself towards the light, as an involuntary pledge of dependence and adoration to the magnificent light. And in response, it travels from your unfolded fingernails down through your fingers, to your arms and into your whole body. You can feel your entire self now smile with the glee of acceptance and honor. You wonder what has happened. And as soon as you internally ask that question, you receive an answer. It's difficult to comprehend, although you hear it distinctly. You understand the content, but it's not feasible. You also understand that soon, you will be back to your normal self. But for now, in this new experience which you will never forget, you are the Christmas cactus plant in your living room, now in full bloom.

Now, you finally wake up back in the real world. Then you thankfully laugh at your strange dream. Wow, you're glad that's over. You take a deep breath and stretch your limbs for a moment, enjoying the movement. What a stressful night that was, as if you didn't have enough stress in your life with the new project at work. Then, it occurred to you. The Christmas cactus actually requires stress to bloom. It must be placed in full sun close to the window glass so that it will experience not only the sun's warmth during the day, but also, and very importantly, the cold of night. Else it simply will not bloom.

You wonder for a second or two, why you had such a dream? Then you remember when you drifted off to sleep last night, you were thinking about (and stressing over) the project. Did maybe your stress messages reverse directions too, and fabricate this dream as a type of nourishment to remind you that people often may need stress to fully bloom too? Think about it.

~ ~ ~

Why this word YOU is important

You must look after the whole precious YOU, to guard and protect your uniqueness and the gifts that you have been given, and also to prepare and enable yourself to reach the best that God has planned for you. God gives us passions ambitions and talents. But we have to un-wrap the package and prepare it for service.

Unwrapping your package means discovering what's inside of you. What are your passions? What are your talents and skills? You must make strong and continuous efforts to discover yours, write them down, update them, study them, practice them and consider how you might use them in life through a selected field of endeavor to serve other people. Whatever your passions, the tendency as gleaned from personal histories, is that the quality of your life will have a definite correlation with how well you activate your passions, talents and skills for your chosen career. That correlation also depends on how well you prepare yourself to fully utilize your passions and talents.

If you had a passion for football, but as a youngster didn't pursue getting on every team you could, and didn't practice over and over and more, your chances of achieving your passion potentials. The NFL is made up primarily of over-achievers. So too are many, but not all, passioned-personal successes.

Whatever your passions and talents, whether to be a full-time mom, or an engineer, or a heavy equipment operator, if you prepare well to honor your passion potentials (at any age) you are doing a great service for yourself to use the gifts you were given.

~ ~ ~

2 - THE SECOND WORD
"SPIRIT"

This second nature somehow understands the voices of the arts, music, the poetry of life and those divine whispers.

Up From the Engine Room

The engine room is our occupational life, our professional energy, our job-devoted focus, our family-functional priority clock. While in the Engine Room, we do this, we do that, we schedule this, and that, hockey practice, football, baseball, dancing, and whatever for the kids or yourself. Keep focused on activity. This is the engine room. To many, this is life.

Please take a break, often. Leave the engine room, and walk up the ladder, climb the stairs, up to the deck on the outside, to view the sky above, the stars, tree limbs against the sky, with the birds dotting the clouds. What might this do to your perspective? What happens to all of us – when we decide, or have the opportunity to, walk up from the engine room? Find those stairs, that pathway, soon, up. Your human spirit is waiting there.

~ ~ ~

Three Months to Live

Imagine you have just learned from your doctor that you

have about 3 months to live. You wander, stunned into a park and drop down on a wooden bench in despair. A youngster about 6 years old strolls up and stares at you. Apparently, drawn to your radiating gloom, the youngster sits down beside you. You notice that the youngster looks a little bit like pictures of you at that age. You wonder what you might share with this youth about life. Suppose that youth is you? What would you tell yourself back then? Maybe what to avoid, what to cherish, what to seek? You wonder too about the differences between what you might advise now versus what actually is being absorbed through this young person's and your earlier societal, educational, home and environmental systems. In your own personal gloom you wonder when this young person will discover the inner spirit, and when it will be needed so desperately, like you do yours right now.

You remember so many times when your much younger inner spirit knocked at your heart's door, asking you to come out and play. But you were too busy. Now, it appears that most, but not all, spiritual transformations begin later in life, or following a crisis (of which "later in life" may also qualify). How unfortunate this is, as many years of blind energy are often spend chasing nothings, counterfeit rainbows projected onto individual screens by our culture, our instructional systems, economic and political infrastructure. You wonder now, how might the process of awakening or spiritual transformation be stimulated earlier, much earlier?

We may have been led to believe that one's spiritual awakening is directly proportional to maturity (usually age). Yet, from birth to early childhood, children already possess a sparkling spiritual quality within their personality. The seed is there. We see this in children's art quite clearly. I remember when one of our grandsons was five years old and drew a tractor trailer truck. It hung on our refrigerator for years. It didn't "look like" a truck – but it "felt like" one. It was pure graphic poetry.

Unfortunately most children soon learn through our fashions and culture to begin disregarding their intuitive fresh and creative art expressions in favor of that which is popular. So many will start to count the wheels, and soon the spiritual poetry of one's art may be lost until possibly they are awakened again, some, many years later, maybe even after living out a culture-prescribed filtered reality.

As we become "educated," we tend to learn to be "real", but not necessarily of reality. We learn violence too, exemplified by teen murders being triggered simply by an unintentional insulting glance. We build day-to-day workplace prisons which promote the disregard for human values in favor of short-term corporate profits. We develop "spiritual black holes" within our human models which may last a lifetime.

Spiritual black holes loom like gravitational black holes. They manifest their high density characteristics when spiritual evolution and universal love becomes so internally compressed from its original implanted seed that the outward radiation of love, like light, simply cannot escape. As the compression intensifies, it propagates a self-sustaining paralysis suspending all natural evolutionary spiritual growth and love manifestations until the infirmity is either interrupted (as by crisis) or it runs its course (as "later in life" gets closer). But, in the meantime, it becomes more contagious than our most dreaded diseases, and it spreads by non-contact osmosis, cultured by our sociological and educational institutions and fostered in families of violence and broken relationships.

You wonder. Perhaps if our strongest early defense against this and our staunchest offense for a youthful spiritual kindling and/or transformation is first and foremost, one's family. Next, one's second family may evolve from the faint whispers from good friends, coupled with active work and efforts from a few non-dogmatic religious organizations. Yet, as good as these are, we're still missing the target by about 30 or 40 years, because so many people are not discovering their passions and purpose until their late 40's and 50's instead of their late teens.

And, while we think about these crucial issues, we (in the USA) allow and enable political ignorance to ban spiritual meditation in public schools. The spiritual black holes become denser as that message is digested by students and their families. By allowing and often encouraging this public deprivation of spiritual knowledge and practice, we are in fact contributing to one of the highest forms of abuse possible.

You look back at the youngster still sitting by you on the bench. Many challenges are ahead. For both of you. What would you tell yourself back then?

~ ~ ~

Not Expected to Live

Preface to this essay: This was written in 1996 when our first (of just two then) grandsons was six years old. We now have 14 grandchildren, and whose stories and family experiences are interwoven (mostly invisible) throughout the 12 Words here.

I have a grandson, age 6, who had a extremely traumatic birth. He was born with a hole in his diaphragm about the size of a tennis ball. Because of that, his lungs would not function. He was breathless at birth. The doctors held little hope for his survival. And, although none with his condition had previously survived at this major metropolitan hospital, they decided to call in a specialist who had just accepted a new position in New York. He agreed to travel to Virginia to perform a very delicate operation to reposition most of his internal organs which had pushed up into his chest cavity, and to close the hole in his diaphragm so that his lungs might work. The operation went surprisingly well, although long term survival was still a big question. Six weeks later he went home. Last Saturday, he played his first little league baseball game. He was a miracle child -- and still is.

During the last six years, I witnessed some most unusual characteristics in this little guy, and I have often wondered if traumatic birth has been associated with unusual insights or personalities. We know, for example, *(See Word 1)* that many plants require stress in order to bloom, such as the Christmas cactus springing from a proportional darkness and exposure to cold, and a slightly too-dry soil. Might human births with extreme stress perhaps cause a similar reaction, or absorb some of what we know as a near-death experience?

Bubby, as we call him, continues to be is one of the most caring young men I know. (I know I sound like a granddad) Other kids are drawn to him. When he was 5, I remember one early morning when he was riding with us to a Saturday breakfast meeting with the family. As we drove up and across the crest of a long hill, he looked out of the windshield with my wife and I and announced (in his words)..."Look at the smoke (fog) and the lights way down the road there. That's neat."

The scene was, as adults might say, moderately moving. But for a 5-year old to observe it, in sort of a spiritual way, was quite surprising to us.

There have been other examples. Another is his art work. Since a very early age, he has always drawn "birds-eye" views of events. This is very unusual for a child. After attending my daughter's wedding rehearsal dinner with us, he sketched the next day a view from above of the entire layout of the place. He had never been there before, but there were the service tables, the one for the snacks on the brick patio. There were all of the tables, the walkways through landscaping, and certain pieces of sculpture – all sketched in children's art, and in his view-from-above perspective. He could explain the function of each.

I have often wondered if he possesses some form of special connection, or near-death memory that goes back to his birth experience. He may have observed his first bird's-eye view as his spirit hovered near the ceiling, watching his beginning, while his breathless body-form laid waiting on the operating table.

So, what might we learn from such difficult experiences? Are these more examples of the Christmas cactus blooming when just the right amount of uncomfortable difficulty and stress is present? Are these invitations to the human spirit to rise to the occasion and participate?

~ ~ ~

Chuck and Cynthia

Cynthia encircled his neck with her outstretched arms. Chuck melted, again, and hugged her against him, while they silently exchanged their marvelous and divine feelings for each other, traversing energy, love and spirits' delight.

It was love at first sight for him, 3-years ago. She was just learning his language. And, even though she didn't even notice him for almost a year, she had always been very special to him and so different than the other females in his life. She always radiated love, for him and for everyone she met. She was truly an angel, to him. Yes. She is Chuck's precious 3 year old daughter.

~ ~ ~

Half-Time Chronicles

A Monday night football dialog-essay between Jeb and Cris

Two former college football player buddies, Jeb and Cris, have been meeting regularly every Monday night during the season to watch the TV football game. Back in college, Jeb was the quarterback and Cris was a wide receiver. Part of the magic between them is their difference in personalities, yet their ability to respect and communicate with each other, just as they did on the field in college. Jeb has a tendency to work out his feelings and beliefs mostly in solitude, while Cris finds it easier to get in touch with his deeper self among people, mostly his sports friends, like Jeb. Tonight, they got into a discussion about peace and quiet, and then God. Here's how it went.

Cris: I just don't see how taking camping trips deep in the woods alone can be fun. To me it would be boring, not to say even a little scary. Suppose you came across a bear?

Jeb: You'd be surprised at how much one can communicate with wild animals just by looking into their eyes. Showing them with your eyes that you are going to give them plenty of room, and not harm them, usually does the trick.

Cris: Doesn't sound like fun to me.

Jeb: It's a good time and place to get in touch with nature.

Cris: How do you get in touch with nature? It's just trees and weeds and stuff.

Jeb: It's all part of our huge cosmic systems which has been assembled for our use and enjoyment -- and responsibility. It's the same as the interior of your car, which you treasure. This is just a whole lot larger.

Cris: I know you hold a special place in your heart for nature, the stars, and stuff. What do you see in those things?

Jeb: To me, they're fingerprints of God.

Cris: Are you sure there is a God?

Jeb: Absolutely.

Cris: How's that?

Jeb: Well, it took me a number of questioning years to come to that conclusion, but after seriously looking at the biggest picture that I as a human could see, it became very obvious -- even logical.

Cris: So, what did you see in that biggest picture?

Jeb: First I saw amazement that there is in fact a big picture for all of us to view and study. It's there, but most of us don't take the time or minor effort to bring it into focus.

Cris: Give me some examples.

Jeb: The first notion of "something out there" that got my attention was simply a question. You know, we are accustomed to accounting for and explaining everything in life. We think we have most things figured out. Take that wall over there for example. We know what is on the other side, don't we?

Cris: You mean the hallway?

Jeb: Yeah. So, the space in this room and in the hallway is within our realm of understanding. And, we generally take it for granted. The entire universe is like a huge room. Humans don't know how large it really is. In fact we don't even know if it has any limits, like a wall to define it. The question that sort of put me in my place is, whatever the size of the entire universe, where ever the edge is -- then, what is on the other side of that edge. What is beyond that?

Think about that for a moment. That blows my mind. But the limit is actually in our heads. We can't understand a room that doesn't have any edges, can we? A room so large that if we walked to the apparent edge of it, that it would just keep getting larger. And, even if we could find the edge, our human mind can not grasp what is on the other side of that edge. The edge for us is our own human limits to grasping a picture so large that it never ends.

To me as a human that mystery is unacceptable and certainly humbling. We must find the answer. But, we never will. At least not while on earth. Even as a goldfish looks up at a jet plane flying above, and acknowledges the movement, it will never understand how the jet engine works, or that people are actually sitting inside the plane. Its mind is not built to handle such a capacity. We are like goldfish looking up at the sky.

Cris: So, that makes you believe there is a God?

Jeb: That makes me realize that there is much more out there and connected to down here than we ever imagined. It makes me realize that we can't use our limited minds to try and figure out what we don't have the capacity to understand. We must use other higher capacity tools to try and scope it out.

Cris: Like what?

Jeb: Our spiritual mind.

Cris: Awe come on Jeb. Now, you've already jumped into religion. I'm still back at the edge of the universe...

Jeb: Our spiritual mind is not religion. Our spiritual mind, which is actually located in our heart, is simply another part of us which we don't use very often. It can't do arithmetic, but it can communicate with a buddy in Iraq who just got injured...even before the notice has been sent out. Scientists call it non-local particle communication, and they have proven that it works, whatever "it" is. Animals, fish and fowl all use similar built-in spiritual equipment connected to their own unique radar abilities to find their way back home. We don't understand and probably never will, so we brush it off as instinct. It is, of course, instinct. It is instinct which uses a spiritual engine to "see" beyond what can be seen physically -- and which still is not religion. Are you with me?

Cris: Yeah, I think so, but how does God fit into this?

Jeb: First let's change God's name for a moment. Then, we will change it back to God later. Right now, let's call God "The Universal Mind." Okay?

Cris: Well, I'm not following you again, but go ahead.

Jeb: The next question that I faced in my questioning period, was did all of this, the universe, humankind, instinct, the spiritual mind, and much much more -- did all of this just happen by accident? Or is there some sort of creative intelligence distributed throughout the universe, which propelled evolution as we know it, and still does? To make a long story short, after reading and questioning much on this, I could not conceive that life, the universe and all of its near miracles simply happened by chance or accident. Even using the laws of chance, it would be essentially impossible for such to happen that way. I suggest you study this process yourself, as many have. Eventually I came to the conclusion, also as many have, including many scientists, that the universe is dynamic. It's driven by a type of intelligence. There is some form of a universal mind behind so many improbable accidental miracles of creation. My spiritual mind confirms this as a type of "knowing".

Our spiritual minds have a gifted ability to actually communicate with that universal intelligence...through osmosis of silent energy. It's almost like you and I on the field. When you are running a pass pattern and are supposed to break to the right, and I see the defenders around you -- somehow, I just know that you are going to break to the left. So, I throw the ball there. Remember that first touchdown against North Carolina in 85?

Cris: Yeah, sure do.

Jeb: And, when you broke left, you knew the ball would be there, didn't you?

Cris: I guess I did.

Jeb: That's the type of communication I'm talking about. We can communicate with the universal intelligence much the same way. Our spiritual mind is the first to discover this. Now, my logical mind agrees. Yes, there is an universal intelligence. We in our culture, following ancient scriptures, choose to call this universal intelligence God. It is not a person, but is like the edge of the universe -- way beyond our capacity to understand. Like electricity, we can't explain it, but we know from its behavior and our reaction to it, it is there.

Cris: Well, I guess I'm not there yet, but I can see what you mean. Maybe my logical mind is almost there, but my spiritual mind, if I have one, is apparently not talking yet.

Jeb: Or, maybe you haven't yet tuned in to your spiritual mind, because there is too much noise. Your logical mind is shouting, our culture is shouting, with all of its commercials, peer pressures, cell phones and eager efforts to achieve peace through vehicles which don't deliver peace. Your spiritual mind is awakened in quiet, like being in the woods, or alone on the beach in the early morning.

Cris: I'll have to admit, there is very little quiet in my life.

Jeb: That's where I sense God's fingerprints and presence the most -- in quiet and among His works in nature. There are so many of God's fingerprints around us. If you have ever seen the sun rise over the ocean, you may have noticed the brilliant colors in the sky, awakening birds flying overhead, the sense of love that outpours from that "good morning" and the near sacred difference that event is from our man-made events. Fortunately my logical mind is bored to sleep, while my spiritual mind is energized in communication.

Cris: I guess I have never actually "participated" in a sunrise.

Jeb: That's a good way of explaining it, Cris.

Cris: Well, maybe I'm feeling a little better about some of this.

Jeb: Hey, half-time is about over. Now the Chiefs are going to make their famous comeback again.

Cris: Yeah, you wish. Well, how do the Bible and Jesus fit into all of this?

Jeb: We're still on for next Monday night, right?

Cris: Yeah. That's when the Redskins whip Dallas, right?

Jeb: See? You're into prayers already. Ha! Okay, next week let's talk some about the Bible and Jesus.

Cris: You're on, old buddy.

~ ~ ~

Preface: When I was 5, we lived next door to a family who had an outdoor goldfish pond. I spent many hours there, in wonder.

The Goldfish

He swims in the moonlight, bright.

glittering in the small pond.

Then stops, poised with a stare,

looking up at me, making contact as

if he knows me and my world.

Staring motionless, almost to smile,

is he wondering what's up here?

Beyond his world of containment,

where wrestling for food is

his single care. Poor little one.

How can he even question

our life, airplanes, or cars,

and certainly not about me?

Up through his watery veil,

yet he still stares, until

our eyes meet again, then

he darts away confused,

his world a blessing to

his friends of the pond.

How can he wonder about me?

I glance away up at the moon,

among the neighboring cosmos.

through my veil of human warp,

and wonder about this place,

its endless space and stars. Yet,

how can I question now what

I see, but can't comprehend?

~ ~ ~

Sunrise at Nags Head, NC

My eyes crave morning's nativity,
birthing another painting of light
on cosmic canvas, stretched sky-tight,
beamed so bright, I watch not for long.
But today it was an enduring sight.

Yawns glowed yellow the horizon,
giving low banded clouds a lens
over the squint line which separates
darkness from dawn -- sky from sea
and yes, feathers from fins.

The sun then peaked deep red-orange,
and domed "hello" as it lifted, holy
behind the lens in celestial disguise
echoing again that glimpsed glory of
the nativity's natal, oh so slowly.

Then as if, having shone that point,
it climbed above the clouds and me
and fired its burning vibrancy,
into billions of glistening mirrors,
now skimming across the sea,

riding color rays from its huge crown
of beaming light and the blazing ball.
dancing in aligned paths, up and down,
swishing like intercessory brush strokes,
now smiling a "Good Morning" to all.

~ ~ ~

When Blossoms Sing

(May be sung to Beethoven's hymn,
Joyful, Joyful, We Adore Thee)

Did you catch the blossoms singing,

In Son's radiance, bright as day?

Did you glimpse too, petals ringing,

His prayer as He would they say?

For blooms commune on cosmic springs

Coiled in Earthen stems so tall,

Stretching for the Light beyond wings,

Aligned, beaming Heaven's call.

While receptors, yaw here and sing,

Absorb, feed, transform and grow,

Grace us in the Light of our King,

Ignite us now, set the glow.

So rejoice in garden's seed time,

When blooms sing Love from the pew,

And the Lord's Prayer, sung in soul's chime,

Plants joys new, to shine through you.

~ ~ ~

Why this word SPIRIT is important

Your spirit resides in your heart not your head. Imagine golden strings attached to your spirit then extending beyond you and connecting with God's spirit. These golden strings carry millions of message every day, including messages of hope, suggestions, warnings, guidance and absolutely great ideas. But you have to turn the switch on at your end.

Imagine for a moment that you are a cell phone capable of receiving e-mail and text messages. Imagine that all of your e-mail goes to your brain, and all of your text messages go to your heart. These two forms of communication are separate and use separate passageways within you, which as you may know is also true of cell phones. Now imagine that text messages are spirited messages, which your heart as the seat of your spirit, understands while e-mail messages are mundane and on a level the brain can easily understand. But the brain cannot hear or understand the spirited message to the heart.

To ignore all of your text messages because you have not yet activated that part of your cell phone is to miss out on all of the possible messages aimed at you through this mode. As any "texter" or "spiritual" person will tell you, that would be a real catastrophe.

To activate your spirit center means primarily recognizing you have it. Then, every time you sense that you may have a non-mundane message coming in, your spirit center turns on automatically. Some people call these non-mundane messages nudges. What do you call them?

I've been told that God does not use e-mail primarily because the brain is not high speed, nor capable of understanding his language, or music, or poetry, or art, or other carriers of his messages. So he uses the human spirit to catch and route his messages (nudges) to you. Your spirit is very important to you. Have you activated and nurtured that part of you?

~ ~ ~

"DREAM"

Dreams, one of the powers which
persuades hope of what might become.

Tugs on the Kite String

As a boxing fan, I always grin at the ringing of the final bell after a 10 round bout, when the two who have been hammering each constantly, stalking, aiming, striking and attacking the other with their toolkits of skill and strength -- then suddenly embrace with joy and respect of the shared experience. For a moment it seems like an illusion, doesn't it?

Comparing seeming illusions in life has a similar ring to it. When the final bell sounds, I suspect that we might understand and respect each other's illusions better. In the meantime, I am reminded of a story I read of a young boy flying a kite high into the air. Soon, the kite disappeared behind low-hovering clouds, and as a friend passed by, he asked, "What are you doing?" The boy replied, "I'm flying a kite." The friend said, "No you're not. I don't see a kite anywhere." The boy responded, "I know it's there. I can feel the tug on the string."

It's difficult sometimes for us to share the tug on our own string, but we all know it is there. That's what dreams do. Is it an illusion? No. Not to us. As Prospero says in Shakespeare's "The Tempest": "We are such stuff as dreams are made of." And, in the simple tune, "Row, row, row your boat," the good news is that, "life is but a dream."

I enjoy hearing about the tugs on other people's strings. That's when you start to see the glow in their eyes. It helps me understand a little bit more about those tugs on mine. It convinces me more too, not to let go of what I feel, what I sense, and what I know is there, but to cherish it more and continue to build my next steps accordingly. I hope you will do the same.

While each of us may perceive our being as both a single wave in the ocean, and an undiluted part of the whole, both offer the ongoing opportunity, as a wave of the whole, to experience those ever-breaking white-laced tips cresting our ride, offering brief peeks below the surface. Peeks into the realization of one of your dreams. What magnificent views!

~ ~ ~

It's Your Choice

Preface. This is an article I wrote in 2010 to help shine a little light on 8 areas for young folks and their families to keep in mind when considering colleges and life careers. It speaks to several of the 12 Words here including dreams.

I remember my senior year in high school when everyone seemed to know exactly what they wanted to do, where they wanted to go to college and importantly, what career course(s) to pursue in college. Well, I didn't know any of that stuff, and I feared for my life. Now 55 years later, retired and a grandfather, I sense again through our growing family of 14 grandchildren, those same high school and college wonderings. What should I do? Where should I go? I fear for them now. Yet, one of the benefits of retirement is the ability to look back, not only to help us in retirement continue to ask and answer those questions for ourselves, but to also help others in younger generations explore and eventually answer for themselves those critical questions. Throughout those 55 years, I made my share of mistakes and paid dearly for some of them, but I also made a number of very good choices, navigated a few U-turns, and generally caught myself just before it was too late (it never is) with much help from God, and I'm still amazed at the journey. Overall if I were to do it all over again, I would keep a summary of eight suggestions in my "iPod."

1. <u>When considering jobs or careers or colleges - start with YOU first and not with jobs, careers or colleges</u>. If you don't really know YOU, then the search will be based on false assumptions. And, when we don't have good clear feelings about upcoming decisions, we tend to bring up and listen to artificial stuff, don't we? In this case, I remember, suggestions from others like, where's the best money? Which courses are the easiest? Which career pathways have the best benefits? Dangerous questions.

Later I learned that such questions are phony and more likely to entice one to become trapped in a "plastic" career which may be meaningless, empty of passion, and void of those joys of deep dedication. Remember reading stories about doctors, lawyers and others who gave up their medical practices or other professional careers, and businesses at age 45 to <u>pursue what they always wanted to do</u>? Ever wonder why they wasted 27 years of career time to learn it was not for them? I continue to wonder why our high schools don't better prepare us to make successful career decisions? Starting with YOU means to truly get to know your talents, passions, dreams and current weaknesses.

2. <u>Then, work from the inside outward, not the other way around</u>. In my case, I was luckier than wise. My school counselors apparently didn't have time to see me, thankfully. Also, my family was poor financially, yet very rich in wisdom and love, and I continue to be so grateful for that magnificent combination of benefits. To help finance my personal needs, I invested in working full time every summer, holidays and even more when possible. That gave me the opportunity to start from

within. I accepted those facts with admittedly less joy then than now. Yet, little did I know that such a "necessity" pathway would spring forth the need and joys of invention, creative problem solving and an awakening of enlightenment beyond all possibilities I could have ever imagined. It was through those job experiences, cutting grass, delivering newspapers, repairing my own bicycles, plus the opportunities of making wrong decisions and then being left 100% accountable (thankfully) for the consequences, that I was able to secure a genuine personal focus and begin to learn true and valuable lessons of life. Don't misunderstand me here though. My parents did not walk away from me or any of my siblings. They watched us like a hawk, while using their exquisite loving parenting skills to guide us, often invisibly, to learn how to learn. Then as siblings we all learned together how to fly like a young hawk.

3. <u>Agree with yourself that this is an on-going process of discovery -- of how and through which fields and venues you will become the most skilled, motivated, effective and whole person in life.</u> I remember learning at age 16 how engineering offices function, all through a part-time job with my consulting engineer Sunday school teacher. Although my duties were primarily drawing ink borders around large blank engineering drawing sheets and re-waxing floors in off hours, but, more importantly I learned the culture and feasibility of a very productive engineering office. I also learned about their primary clients, architects, what they do and how they do it. That simple part-time, bottom of the pay scale job opened my eyes to what eventually became my career in architecture.

As I reflect back, I am eternally grateful that I had to seek my answers through life's experiences rather than trends and trivial social guidelines which so often are not only false but also an immensely dull trap into nothingness. The process of seeking is in itself very healthy, yet often a missed opportunity in today's instant gratification scene. I thank God for the challenges and difficulties placed before me as I grew, and I thank my parents over and over for making me accountable for my decisions. One such stands out. That is when I traded our family power lawn mower, plus some of my own savings, for a used motor scooter. All during that transaction, I could see nothing else other than me riding that beautiful old scooter. My dad, upon learning of the then already-made transaction, thought a moment, then he simply asked me how I would now cut the grass. He didn't ask how are "we" going to cut the grass. I now had a new problem which I certainly should have thought of before. This surely required some innovative thought, and my dad smartly left it entirely up to me. You see, soon I was back in the yard cutting business, initially with our family "push" mower, then with a borrowed power lawn mower, then with a new power mower. That was a valuable lesson I learned through my dad's loving gift of accountability. Accountability is not a punishment. It is a valuable learning opportunity. Yes, unfortunately, too many parents deprive their children of that precious opportunity by bailing them out from all their difficulties.

4. Focus on discovering your passions. Everyone has at least one passion for a "gifted" activity. Some people may be "born" salespeople. They can sell ice to Eskimos. Thus they have a selling talent which could help them significantly in a sales career. Others love intricate detail, numbers, processes - and may be attracted to accounting or engineering activities. Others may have a passion to teach, while others may have a passion for art, or music, or the outdoors. Now imagine putting these passioned (a new word which is better than passionate) people as described above into a "wrong" career match. We would never do that, you might say. However, that is happening, every day. Whether it's caused primarily by parental pressure, peer pressure, inadequate education and guidance, or enticing benefits and salary, people are walking into career traps every day as the first step of a long,

boring, expensive and emotionally painful experience. Some will get out sooner than others and start over again. Cheers to them.

Help on discovering one's passion(s) should start early in high school. This effort should not be diluted through an elective course, but instead included in required courses. But most public educational systems apparently don't consider the process of making life-career choices that important. So, until they eventually "get it" you will have to proactively seek your own sources. But hey! The latest Google search I did for "finding your passion" found 38 million hits in .27 seconds, 38,800,000 hits to be exact. When searching Amazon.com for the same subject, it revealed four pages of books, many of them for less than $12. Writers, individual educators, counselors, coaches and passioned teachers are recognizing this huge personal need in all of us. There are also many books, courses and offerings on similar titles of essentially the same subject. For example, a search on "finding your purpose," or "finding your calling," or "finding your spiritual gifts" will reveal a similar huge popularity and a growing thirst to learn how to find this fundamental meaningful key to one's life. How long will it take for public educational systems to wake up to this? Depends on how much fuss you and others raise over it.

I have studied this subject for years and have found that one of the reasons I like the work processes of architects, goes back to an experience I had when I was 12 years old. As I wrote in my book about clues to highly engaging architecture, that day on a vacant lot next to our rented house, I helped a young stranger fly his kite with the rest of us neighborhood guys. Suddenly his kite crashed and became entangled in power lines. He screamed in horror. Strangely I had the notion that I could do the impossible – by freeing his kite from the wires. As my logic-blinded urge guided my kite over to the power pole, a puff of wind pushed my kite into his, and his kite loosened and then drifted to the ground.

I was just as surprised as the little guy. He picked up his kite and ran over to me with great joy beaming from his face. As I prepared to say, "You're welcome," it was as if someone had then flipped a switch -- and everything appeared to be happening in slow motion. There was no sound. There was only the look on his face of extreme appreciation through a very staggering connection in his eyes. In a few moments, he was gone, and I never saw him again. Throughout my architectural career after seemingly incidental assistance activities for clients, staff and sometimes other architects attending my seminars, I would see that same haunting facial expression and connection again. Each time after a moment of regaining my breath, I viewed such as a hint that I was hopefully on the right track for service. For assisting others, sometimes in breakthrough moments, is definitely one of my passions. I urge everyone to study, explore, read, involve friends, and proactively discover your personal passions. Then build your life around what you can do best for others through those passions. That will be your very special winning combination.

5. Agree with yourself that as you begin to sense your "niche(s)" in studying and serving through your passions and certain field(s), that income levels will follow your zest and skills; and your zest and skills will follow your true passions, plus your extra efforts (which you will enjoy) to highly tune your skills. Follow the biographies of famous and wealthy (if you wish) people. You will find that a majority of them will attribute their successes to doing exactly what they simply love to do -- or as some describe it, serving the purpose for which they were gifted in this life.

6. Then, when evaluating colleges, consider primarily two questions:

   a) Academically which college(s) have the highest rankings in your passion-field(s)?

b) Environmentally and socially which colleges appear to you to <u>best nurture and support physically and emotionally</u> your on-going process of becoming the most skilled, effective, motivated and whole person you are passioned to be?

If you can find a college which ranks very high with you in *both of these areas*, you have found a gold mine.

7. <u>Focus on a wide range of in-process work experiences.</u> When your friends or your children or grandchildren reflect their curiosity and questioning about "What should I do?" or "Where Should I Go?" consider it a great opportunity for them. Adults should generally stay out of trying to provide answers for them. Instead, we should guide them, as early in life as possible and through loving opportunities to explore the real world through meaningful part-time jobs in areas of their passion(s).

If actual employment cannot be secured in the passion areas, seriously look into ways they can work in the passion areas as an intern. Students working for free in areas of one's passions will tend to receive more benefits than working for money in areas disconnected from their passions. For example, if a student with talents and passions in marketing cannot find a part time job in a marketing or advertising company, he/she would tend to be better advised to serve as an intern in such a company than working for pay in an engineering firm.

8. <u>Stay open for mid-course corrections</u>. Listen for nudges and wonderings from your inner self. Be aware of outside nudges too for what might appear to be simple coincidences. If certain nudges keep coming back to you, it may be your inner pilot trying to get your attention. The term "mid-course correction" was coined by the space industry referring to, for example, a space ship's original launch and a trip to the moon. Even though technology provides extreme "aiming" accuracy in the initial launch, the space ship's built-in guidance systems, tuned to both

the moon (the goal) and the launch station (parents), it still needs to make tiny alterations to its course all along the way.

All of us need to make those same mid-course corrections all along our way as we explore, discover and work hard to ratchet up our zest and skills to land within those fields where we will become the highly capable, effective and whole person in life we were passioned to be. Have a safe trip and remember to enjoy the exciting ride.

Now here is a word or two to my "re-tired" friends. This means changing the definition of that term, retired. I like a fresher definition. Imagine a NASCAR vehicle racing around the track. After a while, it pulls into the pits. The crew rushes out to add fuel and change all of the tires. Within seconds, the car races back on the track. It has now been "re-tired" with four new ones, and is back on track. Retirement is a great re-tire opportunity for us to make more mid-course corrections to fine tune our skills and our aim to serve through our passions. Now we can even be an intern again to practice this and share what we have discovered during all of these years. Hope to catch some of you on the next loop around the track.

~ ~ ~

Why this word DREAM is important

Perhaps most of us have heard stories of folks asleep being awakened in the morning by the wonderful aroma of bacon cooking in the kitchen. Or, maybe it was the aroma of biscuits baking or waffles. To me those aromas are like dreams. They carry powerful suggestions and flashbacks of "what can be." In this case they say, "Imagine eating this delicious bacon, or one of these biscuits or waffles?" The aroma makes it almost real; and all we need to do to make it so is take action now, while the beacon and biscuits are still available.

Now a dream to earn and save enough money to buy that car you have always dreamed of contains two enticing aromas. One is from the car, perhaps from riding in one owned by a friend, or the dealer. The interior, the equipment, the power, are all aromas for this car. Wow, I just can imagine me driving this. One day, I will own one just like this one. Dream one is born. I'll need this much money (needs to be exactly specific). Dream two is born.

If those two dreams are nurtured and practiced enough to cause action (earning and saving) chances are very high both dreams will become a reality and the car will be purchased.

Perhaps you've heard the saying, "Be careful for what you wish, because you may very well get it."

Dreams are very powerful two-step processes. They reside in a special semi-private part of the heart which has a two-way thin wire to the brain, plus a major conduit of wires to the rest of the heart where one's spirit resides. The two-way wire to the brain is very important, because that's how the brain and the heart work out the steps to achieve the dream (goal). It takes both types of reasoning, the desire (heart) and the step-by-step (brain) rationale to achieve the goal. It is a joint process of navigating.

To have dreams of what you wish is the first step in navigating. Navigating without a dream is like steering without a map. Without a dream, we drift and are pushed along by someone else's currents as they pursue their dreams. The brain's participation in working out a game plan to achieve the heart's dream is the second step. And, as this chapter suggests: "Dreams are one of the powers (like trust) which persuades hope of what could be." Dreams may also be God's ways of asking, "What do you think? What do you wish for?"

~ ~ ~

4 - THE FOURTH WORD
"GOD"

The silent, fourth dimensioned ever-present intelligence harbors our purpose – and reveals it to each of us once he can get our full attention.

Do You Believe?

Depending on what polls you read, 80% to 90% of the US population believes there is a God. Maybe you're not part of that percentage, yet. Maybe you don't, and won't ever believe. Or, maybe you do, surely and confidently. Wherever you may be in your belief experiences or lack of at this point in your life is okay with me. I will never try to talk anyone into a belief different than what one's experiences suggest is true. Instead, I would rather meet you in this essay wherever you are in your belief experiences and ask you another question. That is, "How did you get there?" Think about that for a moment. You might say, for example, well you were brought up in the church, learned a little bit about religion, God and the Bible, but later you didn't find it contributed significantly to an enhanced life. So you dropped it. Or, you might say you never went to church as a child or since, except at friends' weddings, funerals, etc., and you don't miss religion or any particular belief in a god. You see, my premise here is this: It appears to me that one's belief (or not) in God is significantly influenced by the route one takes to accumulate personal experiences and information to the point of suggesting an answer to the belief question.

As an example, let's consider for a moment how we make decisions about friends, particularly "Very Important People"

(VIP) in your life. Think of your VIPs, maybe a spouse, a girl friend or a boy friend, and/or other close friends. Now, suppose one of your friends volunteers to introduce you to another possible VIP. You say, well okay. Then suppose your friend shows you two blogs that were written by various people about this possible VIP. You read some of both and understand the writings are about people's challenges in life; about the personality of this possible VIP; and about how he helped his friends deal with difficulties.

You noticed in one of the blog summaries that there was an event which separated the two blogs. The event was mentioned as a future occurrence in the first blog. The second and most recent blog reported in greater detail what actually went on during that event. The event was a on-going costume party held over a period of about three years at multiple locations under the theme of life-education for all. This possible VIP was the main speaker at the event. The guests came dressed in all kinds of costumes selected to reflect locations and occupations. Some came dressed as church leaders, some as farmers, herdsmen, fishermen, the poor, and government officials. But the speaker, your possible VIP, appeared every time simply in a costume expertly disguised to resemble most of the guests in everyday life.

"Wait a minute!" You might blurt out. Why all of these behind the scenes descriptions, events, costumes and blogs? Maybe they're important later, but now, I just want to meet this possible VIP, and then I will decide later if he might be a VIP for me. That is exactly the point I wish to make here. Yes, you are correct. Most people would prefer to simply meet possible friends first, get to know him or her, then consider broadening the possible relationship through further meetings, reading about him or her and talking to others about what this possible VIP means to them. That's an effective procedure. But, when one considers the reality of building belief, or disbelief, in God, many people are guided along a different and less-effective route. Instead of trying to meet God or sense his presence first, many people are being routed along a backwards and behind the scenes approach very similar to what I described above. They learn "about" God instead of meeting him..

For example, not-yet-believers are often introduced to the Bible (the two blogs) the Old Testament and the New Testament – and guided to study them to learn about God. This approach tends to skip over or lessen the not-yet-believer's need to experience God's presence and a meaningful spiritual connection first. How can one be expected to make a sound decision on God's relevance to their life if they skip meeting him and personally experiencing his presence – in favor of a type of "library/research" approach? I don't believe they can, honestly. Think about it – God hosted that costume party and became the person, Jesus, in a costume resembling all of us (why?) TO MEET US; to BETTER show us his (God's) personality so that we could better experience meeting him. This "meeting" was God's choice and example to us.

Now, let's consider another story to illustrate the same point. We are going to visit two ice cream stores. Upon entering the first one, you tell the person behind the counter that you are undecided about their brand of ice cream (religion) and particularly their flavors (denominations). The person replies, "Well, you see, the Persians had a type of ice cream in 400 BC, using syrups cooled with snow. Later they mastered the technique of storing ice in giant natural-cooled boxes called yakhchals. Then a mixture of milk and rice was used in China around 200 BC...." This history lesson goes on and on until you put a stop to it.

"Hold it a minute!" You might interrupt the clerk. "That doesn't help me make a decision about your ice cream or which flavor to pick." You walk out of the store, an unbeliever in what this store sells. Then you enter the other store and repeat what you said in the first store – that you are undecided about their brand of ice cream and particularly their flavors. The person in this store replies, "Well, do you see any flavors here in the cases that you would like to taste?" You smile and taste two flavors from a small cup and plastic spoon. Then you decide on a cone of the second flavor. After finishing that, you have enough information/experience to make a decision. You will be back to this store again. It was the tasting that did it -- "meeting" the ice cream.

The history of ice cream may be entertaining, particularly to a bored intellect, but the real-life taste is what we need to make a personal experience decision. Personal experience decisions are anchored to the heart and soul. Intellectually entertaining decisions based on history, rules and dogma are anchored momentarily to the brain, a non-spiritual part of the human body. That same intellect-based process-belief is what powered Saul of Tarsus in his early religious decisions. Saul was an authority on old Jewish law, its dogma and how it should be practiced. Jesus' teachings outraged Saul and his memorized practices of the law. So Saul, a Roman citizen, chased early Christians and had them arrested and persecuted. Then, on the road to Damascus to seek out more Christians, Saul met Jesus' resurrected spiritual image and had a crushing "ice cream tasting experience" with the Holy Spirit. This blinding experience power-blasted Saul's conversion for the rest of his life with unceasing devotion to Jesus and his teachings. Jesus changed Saul's name to Paul, and Paul wrote much of the New Testament throughout his missionary trips and imprisonments.

Do you see now why I asked you the question earlier, "How did you get to your current belief?" Did you sense God's presence first, and then decide you wanted to learn more about him and his ways as revealed by Jesus? Or, were you in your early belief development guided to skip (or delay) trying to meet God and instead focus on reading the Bible and attending church services? Is your decision anchored in your heart and soul, or is it temporarily paper-clipped to your wandering intellect?

In his book, Blended Worship, by Robert F. Webber, Henderson Publishers, Inc. 1996, he wrote in prayer, "God, I don't want more information about you. I want you!"

Well then, how do we get God? How might one meet God and/or experience his presence? Now we're asking the right question, first. How do you find God, not just information about him. My premise suggests that once a person has experienced God's presence through his or her own individual experiences, then Biblical readings, histories, stories, rituals, hymns and fellowships not only nurture that underlying relationship further, but they now will nurture it more powerfully. Once our attitude and awareness are in sync, we can better accept and apply Biblical scripture as our standard of behavior. Reading and studying the Bible now, under this more spiritually-direct routing, helps us align our thinking with God's. Through consistent nurturing we slowly begin to change ourselves from the inside-out in the way we look at things and how we carry that out in our daily living. This is the God's presence approach.

However, to attempt to force an artificial relationship with God through a backwards process using historical and dogmatic conditioning may do more spiritual harm than good, just as it did with the early Paul. Jesus corrected that for Paul, once and for all. So, you may wonder then – why do so many religious programs and institutions choose the weaker and less effective backwards route? They choose that route because it is much easier to deliver and it is readily repeatable. That route, however, experienced initially by spiritual rookies is a very poor one for building deep and lasting faith.

Is this possibly one of the reasons recent Gallup polls confirmed again that Americans' weekly church, synagogue or mosque attendance numbers in 2010 continues to under-perform the 80% - 90% belief in God figures by achieving only about half of that and fluctuating in the range of 42% - 44%? Within that low 40's range, the mega and often alternative programmed churches generally show attendance growth while the smaller and more traditional churches continue to show attendance decline. There are exceptions, but the trends are becoming clearer.

Well then, what are some ways and steps we can explore and use to help us experience God's presence early in our belief development? Select books on this subject. Consider too that God is already here, there and everywhere, unchanging. It is our perception of God which needs assistance. Here are six steps that I have found helpful in awakening and encouraging more insightful perceptions of the presence of God. You are encouraged to explore and develop your own better ways which work for you.

1. Importantly, step outside of your culture for at least 20 minutes each day. Find a quiet place you can go without being interrupted – maybe by the seashore, at a mountain overlook, in a park, or maybe in a quiet room in your house that has a quiet view. Sit there comfortably. Take three deep and slow breaths. Close your eyes and imagine that you are visiting your great-great-great-great grandfather or grandmother (who I will call your G5). Your G5 has no TVs, no cell phones, and none of the many other devices in your current culture. But, God is not in any of those devices anyway. If while sitting there back in time, maybe 200 – 300 years ago, your current culture keeps interrupting you, imagine you pushing it into a closet and you locking the closet door for a while. Consider what your G5 would want for you. Imagine

your G5 praying that for you, and you are over-hearing that. What is your G5 saying? Sit and picture that for a while, now as you say a prayer too. Pray that God will reveal himself to you and give you a sign just prior to that happening. Pray that you will be open to that experience. Then, when you are ready, imagine waving good-bye to your G5 and you moving forward in time to now. You open the closet door, and your current culture steps back into your life. You are back.

2.   In step 1 did you notice the quiet? Did you also notice your inner senses being a bit more aware of things not seen – like your G5? Imagine you have a switch that you can flip on; signaling your personal antenna to sense more clearly those things, thoughts and energies not seen. And, while that happens, the switch also acts like a volume control to turn down distracting noises and interruptions. Consider that you can turn on that switch anytime you wish.

3.   Visit places of God's most beautiful creations. Make a list of your favorite most beautiful and inspiring places. Some of mine include an oceanside or riverside sunrise, inside a room or chapel with multi-colored stained glass, expanses of rolling hills, mountain overlooks and others. The idea is to identify ones that influence you, and then visit those often. While there, flip that switch in step 2.

4.   Visit places where God's presence is known to have been felt before by others. Many of these may not be religious facilities. Google "Inspiring Places" in your area. At this writing I got 1,760,000 results in 0.21 seconds. Some of them have videos of the views, etc. Visit your favorites and turn on that switch in step 2 again.

5.   Ask, seek, and knock. These words of Jesus are found in all three of the Gospels as a key for us. Here is the full verse as found in Matthew 7:7-8 (NKJV) *"Ask, and it will be given to you; seek, and you will find; knock, and it will be opened to you. For everyone who asks receives, and he who seeks finds, and to him who knocks it will be opened.* Putting this in the context of this essay, I must say that this verse is much more meaningful and confirming to me now than it was when I was being coached to simply read the Bible before I had sensed God's presence in my life. This ask, seek and knock is also very good business and communications advice. In both secular and spiritual experiences, this principle makes a good deal of sense. The idea is to be specific about what you are wishing. Don't just say, I want a happier life. Ask specifically for what you wish, then seek it proactively, and knock on a lot of doors to help reveal what you are seeking (and perhaps receiving). In our context here, ask God to reveal his presence to you; and seek that presence rather than just sitting back and waiting for some type of magic to happen. Knock on many doors of possibilities. Do all three proactively, then the real magic will begin…at God's timing.

Now here is an interesting discovery that may entertain your intellect too. **A**sk, **S**eek and **K**nock also forms an acronym, ASK. See? Ever noticed that? I didn't either until my brother brought it to my attention. Most other translations maintain that acronym; though some of them change seek to search, or to seeking. But the acronym holds. Do you think God had a twinkle in his eye when he nudged that ASK acronym to Biblical writers and later to the translators?

6.   Meditate. A Google search of this single powerful word produced 4,890,000 responses in 0.46 seconds. Check it out. Essentially all religions use this practice to enhance spirituality and an oneness with God. Dr, Herbert Benson, Harvard Medical School, clinically studied Transcendental Meditation and found that the process triggers natural human responses which are not necessarily associated with any religious belief. (ACLU, are you listening?) Dr. Benson named the response The Relaxation Response, which is also the title of his book about his study and findings. In it, he shows simple step-by-step instructions for achieving the relaxation response and the benefits. I highly recommend his book. The point of considering meditation here in this essay is that meditation can greatly assist prayer. While the meditative process does not require prayer to work, the process unquestionably nurtures prayer. It opens the mind (and I believe the soul and heart) to astonishing depths of perception and clarity. When you are proactively asking, seeking and knocking, the practice of meditation gives you a near-perfect mind and body environment to sense God's presence.

My practices have shown me that once I experience God's presence in quiet meditation or prayer, or any other way, that reading scripture and daily devotionals then becomes more enlightening, nurturing and rewarding. Such readings and devotionals are then confirmation points as well as new inspirations. I welcome them. On the other hand, without one first building that nurturing underlying awareness and acceptance of God's presence as a prerequisite, I suspect those same scripture verses and devotionals may be perceived by some non-believers as religious commercials. They may be unwelcomed distractions to what we are talking about here. So, one of my "askings" now is that families, churches and seminaries focus more strongly on guiding, and training people to help others experience <u>first</u> the presence of God – as the underlying foundation to help them grow. Oswald Chambers in his <u>My Utmost for His Highest</u> book, published by Discovery House Publishers, Grand Rapids MI, said it this way.

"It is possible to know all about doctrine and yet not know Jesus. The soul is in danger when knowledge of doctrine out steps intimate touch with Jesus. Why was Mary weeping? Doctrine was no more to Mary than the grass under her feet. Any Pharisee could have made a fool of Mary doctrinally, but one thing they could not ridicule out of her was the fact that Jesus had cast seven demons out of her; yet His blessings were nothing in comparison to Himself."

Just as today, it was not the doctrine behind the ice cream in store #1, through which we made our decisions. Rather it was the taste of the ice cream in store #2 that convinced us.

~ ~ ~

God and Good Science

Preface. Sir Isaacs Newton, perhaps the World's greatest physicist pursued physics with a passion. What most people don't know is that physics was his second passion, and that he used physics to reveal the nature of his first passion. God. It's true.

We often hear that "good science" relies on facts, not faith. Yet I respectfully submit that such a broad proclamation is a scientific misnomer. Faith, as a confident belief in the truth of a idea or premise, is used substantially in science, particularly in examining the existence or nonexistence of invisible or directly unobservable phenomena. Science simply chooses to use different words to describe its belief-building process.

An example is the scientifically acceptable process of evaluating possible discoveries of new planets. Often such discoveries are confirmed through a series of observed behavior patterns of nearby known and visible objects in space being exposed to the unknown object/force. Frequently science cannot "see" the unknown object, because of distance or other objects in the line of sight, so it deduces a scientific "knowing" (belief) by observing repeatedly the behavior patterns (wobbles) of seen and known nearby objects by being exposed to the proximity (gravity) of the unseen probable object. Even adding other deductive tools used in combination with this wobble effect measurement, there is still a gap between pure scientific proof of a new discovered planet and acceptable scientific deduction that one does "in fact" exist. The gap is belief, or faith.

In 1927 Werner Heisenberg discovered what is now one of the cornerstones of quantum mechanics, and that is the Uncertainty Principle. A consequence of the Uncertainty Principle is that if a particle's (an example electron's) position is defined precisely, then the momentum of the particle will not be precisely defined – and vice versa. Uncertainty is a given in quantum science – even formulated in its practices. Uncertainty is the shirt-sleeves of belief development. The doorbell to research, both outward and inward. Uncertainty has fueled many scientific discoveries and remains a quantified part of the process.

Another example of science using a deductive "belief" system in its process, rather than only observed and proven facts, is in the confirmation of the existence of black holes throughout the Universe. Scientists know very little about black holes. They are invisible to all known telescopes and cameras. Yet it is believed that black holes are abundantly plentiful in the Universe and perhaps may be part of what holds galaxies like ours together. The density and gravitational pull of black holes are (believed to be) so enormous, that even light cannot escape (bounce back), thus they appear only as black voids. We can measure nearby objects disappearing into the voids over time. Black holes, dark matter and dark energy are believed (through deductive mass calculations) to make up over 75% of the Universe, yet they remain dense mysteries. We cannot see any of them, but scientists "believe" they are there -- and they engineer space probe travel accordingly.

So, what about God? Using the same logic as "good science" one CANNOT prove there is NOT a God, anymore than one as yet can prove that there IS a God. For God is invisible, just as certain new planets, black holes, dark matter and any number of other cosmic mysteries. But Christians and others "know" that God is there, and here, because we continue to measure the affects of known objects (people) when they are exposed to the presence of the unseen object (God) force. We can see the wobbles. We can see the changes in human orbit caused by the unseen object/force when the known objects (people) are brought into historically predictable realms of influence of the unseen object/force, God (or whatever name one may wish to use). Basing decisions on God's existence on sight is a weak premise, just as such would be regarding the makeup of the Universe.

Thus, since one cannot prove that there is NOT a God -- atheism is actually another belief system, a negative faith, and NOT a conclusion of facts. As such, atheism has no more civil rights to demand the disassembly of a manger scene than others have to set one up. For publicly calling for the removal of a manger scene, or a Ten Commandments plaque in public places would then be conjoining one specific belief system within State/Federal public protocol -- which as we know is absolutely unconstitutional.

Instead, all belief systems merit the right to exist and flourish as long as they do not endanger public health and safety, nor prohibit other belief systems from doing the same. This is truly "good science" and what is technically found in the constitution -- buried today behind court pseudo-science and politically incorrect interpretations of civil liberties. Think about it.

~ ~ ~

Next Preface. The writings which follow here come from new lyrics to four hymns I wrote over the years. First, an introduction.

When I think of introductions of God, I am reminded of a story Dr. James Flamming, former senior pastor of First Baptist Church, told in one of his sermons in 1998. Paraphrasing from memory...one morning Dr. Flamming glanced out of a window in his study and noticed a group of birds fretting and fighting over something. After a few minutes, he opened the window and tried to calm them. Then, seeing his efforts being ignored, he tried to scatter them...to allow them time to re-think their ploys. Nothing worked. He sensed that if he could just become a bird, for a moment, he could put himself right in the middle of the ruckus and talk to them...in a language they would understand. Maybe then, they might discern what was happening and come to their senses. Then, he saw the metaphor. How God did just that for us. He, through Jesus, became one of us, right in the middle of the ruckus, to help us understand the meaning of love...and come to our cosmic senses.

What a good story illustrating Jesus' purpose. I liked it so much that I wrote lyrics to a hymn based on the story. It is entitled "Like a Dove Unto Our Flock was Born."

"A Dove Unto Our Flock was Born"
The lyrics below can be sung to "It Came Upon a Midnight Clear."

Might love unto our flock appear,

Among the chatter of fear.
Yea, the keeper of the flock did send
Waves of His love to hear.
But many fell unheard again,
On ears un-captured ring,
Tuned tightly to the will of strife,
So neither did we sing.

The Keeper of the flock did shape
Part of His own like them,
And molded it as a pure young dove,
To land in Bethlehem,
To teach us all, the Keepers song,
In words that soon would bring,
For hearts and souls to hear at last,
How all can merrily sing.

The Dove did teach to all the flock,
From the Keepers un-furl-ed wings,
And some did finally understand,
From boundless love to sing.
Like a Dove unto our flock was born,
From heaven's all gracious King,
And now, through love He sends to all,
The birds can joyfully sing.

~ ~ ~

"God Smiled That Day"

The lyrics below can be sung to most 8.8.8.8 LM metrical hymns.

God smiled that day above the sands,
His sunbeams soaring through the skies,
Gliding earthward to light His plans,
Many would see with their own eyes.

For the God of all – time was near,
To transform His Word from above
To a babe in swaddling clothes here,
And nurture His new plan of love.
A Son's glow will shine upon all
Bursting with love for you and me.
His light will absorb darkness call,
While our pardon hangs on a tree.

We celebrate His joyful birth,
Declared by heaven, willed by choice,
God's greatest gift, Shepherd of Earth,
And Master of how to rejoice.

Yes, God surely did smile that Day,
As grace covered our deaf obey.
Help us still Lord, to live His way.
Birth us again, on Your Son-day.

~ ~ ~

"Celebrate the Gift of Presence"

The lyrics below can be sung to the Hymn
"Come Thou Fount of Every Blessing."

Never in our history records
has a small speck flash in time
blazed with such a loving brilliance,
and burned deep a thousand minds,
than the promised life to measure,
lived to unveil its new song,
still remembered, and so treasured
by so many, for so long,
Yes the Son child held by Mary,
hallowed by God, dawned to hug,

later lived His pristine purpose,
then was murdered by the smug,
but to rise yet, in His essence,
birthed again in our hearts hay.
Celebrate the Gift of presence.
Merry Christmas every day.

~ ~ ~

Why this word GOD is important

All people have the right to believe or not believe in whatever they choose. Depending on what poll one reads, 80% to 90% of those in the USA believe in a supreme intelligence, a God. Various polls including the ARIS poll put the percentage of atheist at .4% to 13.6%, with the higher figure including 13.2% of those who selected the nonreligious/secular group.

While believers generally do not need or seek scientific validation of the existence of God, because their beliefs do not come from that source of experience, I am persuaded that some nonbelievers and proclaimed atheists might be curious about some of the recent scientific insights now published for the non-scientist general public. There's more on this on the next page.

This book does not attempt to convince anyone of any particular belief or non belief, for such is between each individual and his/her deity or absence thereof. I do, however, wish to reveal for believers and nonbelievers information and sources including scientific ones that may assist all in fostering and strengthening discussions, enlightenment and personal choices.

Accordingly, I wonder if some of those who do not (yet) sense God as a silent fourth-dimensional ever-present intelligence of the Universe might consider some of the relatively new "proofs" in science of observable activities all around us which can be described as spiritual in nature. Some of these new scientific revelations are summarized in other parts of this book primarily as additional examples of the splendor and wonder of God's creation. But, such are also included as possible helpful information for groups of believers to understand and share with organizations and third party watchdog groups who threaten the freedom of believers practicing their own faiths.

One of these new revelations of wonder and fact is the quantum physics discovery of paired electrons being separated (even by millions of miles) and yet still evidence the ability to communicate wirelessly with each other, and to do so <u>instantly</u> rather than being limited by the speed of light (as proclaimed by Einstein). Our cell phone communication, for example, is limited to the speed of light. See <u>Leadership and the New Science</u> by Margaret J. Wheatley, Second Edition, Berrett-Koehler Publishers, Inc., 1999. For those interested in further scientific detail in these new (spiritual) discoveries, I am including in the Appendix certain portions from my book, <u>Thin Places and Five Clues in Their Architecture,</u> which illuminates some of Wheatley's fine work.

Believers know that God is important to all of humanity, and we practice that knowing by honoring his presence, love and impact in our lives daily. To us God is a reality and a force of love never to forget.

David, Israel's greatest King wrote of this so well in one of his Psalms 103: 1-2 (NIV).

1 Praise the LORD, O my soul;
   all my inmost being, praise his holy name.

2 Praise the LORD, O my soul,
   and forget not all his benefits.

~ ~ ~

5 - THE FIFTH WORD

"LOVE"

God delivers this lovely flower in abundance and implants it in each of us so we will absorb it and radiate it continually back to God and to others.

One of the best descriptions of love I have found is in the Bible, 1 Corinthians 13:4-7 (NRSV).

Love is patient; love is kind; love is not envious or boastful or arrogant or rude. It does not insist on its own way; it is not irritable or resentful; it does not rejoice in wrongdoing, but rejoices in the truth. It bears all things, believes all things, hopes all things, endures all things.

Perhaps second to God's love, most of us might say our mother's love is/was very close. The month of May was selected to associate with this word "Love" among the other 11, because May usually brings us an abundance of flowers. Another good reason for associating May with love is the occurrence of Mother's Day in May. I still remember that first Mother's Day after my mother died. It was difficult. It was the first Mother's Day in 66 years that I did not have a living mother. For most of those 66 years it was the first Mother's Day that I didn't have a card for her. That thought kept coming back to me. Later I sat down and experienced some of the same feeling I must have felt at a very young age when I made her first card from me. I decided to make her last card from me too, but this one would be different. I wrote a poem to her. I share that with you here hoping that those of you whose moms are still living, and those of you who have lost your moms may all be reminded of her love for you – and yours for her.

"Happy Mother's Day, Mom"

This year my card is different, Mom
With worn pictures taped crooked,
Clinging to frayed pages of memory
Gathered from corners of our kitchen
Deep seasoned with your practiced care.

But the pictures this year chat invisible,
Like the wind across the seashore
Shadowing waves it earlier nurtured
Crayoned violet-blue and white
Bursting aromas Alfalfa and Rosemary
Like the South fields of Red Oak.

Where straw-hatted Grandpa Mullins
Helped me steer Jack, the old mule
Nine feet high – and heavier
Than our white-walled 37 Plymouth,
Thrilling me, to express-learn the ropes
While you guided discoveries within.

I still smell your fried chicken, Mom
And hear the crackling welcomes
Pulling Mrs. Tyler from next door
Never listening to soap operas, she says
But visiting us in balmy spring
When breezes blow neighborly

Through open windows and heart.
Feathering those veiled curtains we
Stretched-dried across pin-riddled frames
While Stella Dallas, episode 748
Echoed from the Tyler Motorola,
Just an ear-throw away.

Yes, this Mother's Day is different, Mom
The first since your October graduation
When Robins sang your favorite hymns,
Your name was called, you took your passport
From your Bible, bookmarked at Psalm 23,
And placed your Bible with your scrapbook
On the table there for all of us.

Then you walked across the white stage
To those waiting open-armed in the wings
Smiling, with Dad, as you held your
Passport high, while all cheered and sang.
Then all of you in white flew back home,
Under the light – the glistening white light.

Happy Mother's Day, Mom.

~ ~ ~

Mrs. Jacob's Story

A 10 year old boy, Jasper, is struck by a stray bullet while
riding his bicycle to his grandmother's house. His frail body falls
across his bike, then onto the street...tumbling against the broken

curbing. He lays motionless with a part of his bike across his legs, his bleeding head twisted against the cold concrete curb. Cars speed by. For moments there is not a sound except the dog barking in the distance.

As Jasper's mind slows down with the loss of blood and the crushing impact of the raging bullet against his skull, he feels no pain whatsoever. New thoughts slowly emerge. A calm peace comes over him as he lies still on the pavement.

Shortly, reporters lean over the still boy. Neighbors lean over too and cry with grief that it happened again. Flash cameras and video beams capture the scene eagerly for the evening news. Then in an unexpected moment, Jasper opens his eyes and stares straight up at the crowd leaning over him.

"Tell them the story," he gasped. "They need to hear the story. Please tell them."

Then, Jasper died.

"What stories?" a neighbor asked, looking up at all of the others gathered around Jasper. "What stories? Tell them to who? What's he talking about?"

`Everyone motioned their heads back and forth. Don't know. Mrs. Jacobs knows. Jasper suddenly finds himself standing with the group of neighbors and reporters gathered around his lifeless body lying on the pavement.

"Someone call 911," old Mrs. Jacobs said. "He's hurt real bad."

She turned towards the Jackson house, across the trash laden street and yelled to them, wherever they were.

"Jessie. Jessie! Call 911 now! Ya hear me?"

Finally, a second floor window opened, and Jessie's son, Gerome stuck his head out and yelled back. "What's going on?"

"Call 911!" Jasper's hurt bad."

Gerome waved his hand and ducked back inside.

Jasper looked over at Mrs. Jacobs, the lady he has known all of his short life. The lady who told him the beautiful story. The lady who used to always overpay him by a dime or two whenever he helped her clean up around her house. She said he hadn't figured it exactly right, and to study real hard on his math.

She stared back at him, but didn't respond to his new presence standing over his own body. Then, Jasper felt a hand on his shoulder. He turned and saw an older man who looked very familiar. "Hi Jasper," he said. "I've come to show you a few things while we head back home. "Look over here," he said.

As he did, Jasper touched your shoulder inviting you to join him in the rest of this story. You start to nod an okay, then in an instant, Jasper and you are off to another location, standing on a wide sandy beach, calm waves lapping against the shore, and the early morning sun glimmering through a heavy mist.

"See that up there?" the old man asked, pointing up in the mist.

"Where?"

"Look there. See it? That little speck floating in the air?"

Jasper saw it. And you see it, a speck of dust...as it drifted slowly through the air, with tiny little particles flickering in the light as it moved through the heavy mist.

I'm going to tell you Jasper and your friend here the same story that Mrs. Jacobs told you about God's world, and the most powerful word he gave us. But I'm going to show both of you the details of it working, right here.

As we begin, notice that the speck is suspended in mid-air, pulled by gravity, yet also escorted by wind, static electricity and many other forces. This little dust fragment has been on its course for some time. It has whisked by the shoulders of one named Suicufnoc then one called Eltotsira and others. So too, in its flight path, did it touch those called Setarcos, Ahddub, and then Susej. And now, it continues on past your shoulders, Jasper, for you and your friend to follow and observe.

Jasper learns that both of you have been granted the extraordinary power to visually zoom in on this little speck, just as if he were wearing microscopic lens in front of his peering eyes.

Both of you try the lens and zoom in to discover what may be riding within this collection of fuzz, each separated from the other, yet embracing some form of alignment, an apparent formation in flight, like a group of birds held together by their spirit of instinct, yet separate and distinguished by a their individual self. But, unlike a flock of birds, whose leader is at the helm, here, the leader particle, it seems, is at the center, with the other pieces of dust saluting its position, like tribal people encircling a crackling campfire, or pedals surrounding a bright red bloom, each honoring the group's noble core.

You two zoom in further and are attracted by a luminescent bluish sub-particle, off-center and one of the smallest fragments in the entire speck. You both learn that this particle is named Htrae by those within the group. And, as you zoom in further, you're both stirred by the beauty of all the encompassing bits within this view. There's thousands of sub-particles, bits of dust, and even smaller bits chasing after each other. Moving still closer, you begin to sense waves of funny energies, seemingly coming from this small particle, energies entrapped mostly out beyond, and even reaching out to us.

Now you can feel the energies stronger, like the invisible heat of a distant flame. Some of these energies emit a faint yet deep feeling of adoration, which we can actually detect, like a fourth dimension variety of gravity, a pull of oneness and ardent harmony. The waves of consonance apparently carry some form of a message that the other particles grasp and somehow understand, because we can now detect a pulsating glow from the Htrae particle...with each wave and in rhythm with slight flickers from the others. You and Jasper wonder...if this cluster of dust is actually some form of living organism. Maybe like a jelly fish? But this is just a dust particle.

Then, you feel other energies, sensations of fear and pain...and deep sorrow. A brief surge of desperation drifts over you two, like a gray cloud moving across a brilliant sunny sky, and for a moment, you experience the pains of murder and hopelessness. Then, there's an intermingling of chaotic yet rhythmic energies...then another gentle ripple of adoration, like a distraught ship sending out static and fuzzy signals to anyone listening. You wonder again...how is this possible? How can there be such messages? You zoom in closer still, to observe more of this miniature grandeur. Now, you see a small reflector disk hovering over the smidgen particle. It looks like a satellite reflector aimed precisely at some target to send and receive information. Jason notices it too. Now, you're close enough to barely see the surface of the reflector, and listen intently with your sensations to the faint pulsations, radiating to somewhere. As you focus on the reflector surface, you can see a mirrored view of Htrae itself in the background, and then its distant neighboring particles beyond within a misty swirling fog.

Then, you see what appears to be – it couldn't be – a human figure. No. There's two of them, an adult holding a child, silhouetted in the reflection. Can't see any face yet, just form. You move closer, and even though you're at an angle, now you can see them more distinctly. You peer ahead and focus at the disk, and then suddenly freeze at what you see. The human figure which you now frightfully recognize, waves back at you, crucially like the occupant on a drifting life raft, with tears pouring over a gleeful smile, waving at you as if you're a welcomed helicopter pilot waves of radiant adoration and desperation. Then, you see another jolting realization. As the particle's name Htrae is mirrored in the surface of the disk, it reads backwards with transformed text: "Earth".

You nearly lose sight of this startling scene, as you now grapple through your own tears and struggle with the revelation, that Suicufnoc then...is indeed Confucius. And, Eltotsira...Aristotle. Then, you sense the touch of their very breaths...as they emerge obscurely beside you now. There's that mystical formation again. There's Socrates, Buddha, Jesus and others, assembled randomly, yet somehow aligned. Several are facing towards each other and some looking off in different directions, but all intrinsically connected through some pivotal composition, like football players in huddle, casually grouped, but uniquely connected through their attention towards the quarterback, relaying signals sent in by the Coach. Here, you sense a similar order with messages emitting as whispers of energy...now radiating beyond you and on towards the view below. You hear their choral-like murmurs, delivered again in a reversed text semblance, but this time with you hear their faint phonetic echoes, repeating serenely again and again. "evol, evol." That's Mrs. Jacob's story. She will tell it again and again. But she spells it the other way around, "Love." Jasper's grin grows wider and wider. Then he moves on with the old man. And, you're now standing back at the crowd hovering over Jasper.

~ ~ ~

Why this word LOVE is important

Love is the glue which holds everything else together. Do you agree? Think about it. Paul of Tarsus writing to members of a new church he started in Corinth put it this way:

"And now these three remain: faith, hope and love. But the greatest of these is love." 1 Corinthians 13:13 (NIV)

6 - THE SIXTH WORD

"FAITH"

The foliage, ahead of the bloom, supports and nurtures the blossom – once the plant is fertilized with relationships of honor and trust.

"The fundamental fact of existence is that this trust in God, this faith, is the firm foundation under everything that makes life worth living. It's our handle on what we can't see. The act of faith is what distinguished our ancestors, set them above the crowd."

Hebrews 11:1 (MSG)

As said back in Chapter 4, contrary to popular belief, faith is used in science as well as life in general. "Faith as a confident belief in the truth of an idea or premise is used substantially in science, particularly in examining the existence or nonexistence of invisible or directly unobservable phenomena. Science simply chooses to use different words to describe its belief-building process."

In life and day-to-day matters we go through similar processes to form our opinions of reality. If an opinion is substantiated over and over through our relationship with a particular aspect of reality, such as the sun rising every morning, we build trust in that happening again. Once trust in that particular situation reaches a level of near certainty to us, we don't hesitate to use a word stronger than trust, such faith. For example, I have faith that the sun will rise again tomorrow morning. Although I have a "knowing" that it will, I don't actually know yet, because tomorrow hasn't happened yet. But in the meantime, that knowing is strong enough for me to make decisions based on that knowing being a reality. I'm going to make plans for tomorrow, and doing so is based on the faith that the sun will in fact rise again. Even if it's cloudy and we can't see the sun, we can see the daylight, so we just "know" that it is there.

If we break down that process of forming such a strong opinion, we'll find that it is a simple three-step process.

1. A relationship is formed with the situation (sunrise). As that relationship continues, certain aspects "prove" themselves over and over. We don't see the sun every day, but we do the daylight, thus seeing the sun every day is not one of the provable aspects. But, daylight is.

2. As that happens again and again, we build a sense of trust in the situation. We eventually trust in daylight happening every day.

3. As that builds sufficiently to unquestionably prove its trustworthiness to us, we now secure our faith in daylight happening every day. We continue in our relationship with the sun rising, now assured of its trustworthiness, which now importantly further enhances the relationship. The loop continues building and enhancing.

Now, we can apply that process to many aspects in life, friendships, marriage, and God. Add love to the recipe, and it will be the glue which will consistently hug and hold the three ingredients together. But skipping any of the three could be like sky diving without a parachute. For faith without experiencing an earlier developing trust may have a slippery foundation. And trust formed in the absence of a maturing relationship, may be better described as gambling. The high percentage of failed marriages serves as an unfortunate example.

~ ~ ~

When Faith Falls

On this September day, when fate
would blast and burn, shriek and stun
with fear veiled even in its date,
staring at us -- its nine, one one,

when silent screams from children's souls
were triggered by those taught to hate,
would reveal their cowardly goals
to annihilate the open gate.

When silent screams -- of those mothers,
fathers, kids, husbands and wives,
would cry out to family and others
of crushed dreams and vanished lives.

When silent screams -- buried and bled
from rage burned deep in our eyes,
-- haunt us now, while we clutch our dead
below the sooted dove, which -- still flies.
The sooted dove still flies.

When faith falls, the sooted dove still flies. The human spirit
with its faith in God, Love and the other 10 words here, will
forever fly. We start over again. One of the first words of these
12 that the human spirit recovers is faith – our spirit's engine of
being.

~ ~ ~

The Engine of Being

(A prayer)

Was it that nudge

I failed to feel,

that push, Lord,

I didn't sense was real?

Was it your voice

I failed to hear,

which whispered

paths so near?

Was it that crash

I failed to see,

your acts of wisdom,

and special will for me?

Yet, now I know, Lord

it is through all of these,

which opens my heart

and buckles my knees.

Thanks to you, Lord, for prodding,

for listening and seeing,

for nurturing seeds of faith,

our spirit's engine of being.

Thank you, Lord, for fresh pathways,

where times and efforts interlace,

where plans are tugged by your will,

and tweaked by angels in grace.

Help us, Lord, reside in your light,

singing not ours, but your song,

with twelve voices and work ahead,

for there's where our hearts belong.

Amen.

Why this Word "FAITH" is important

It is fourth down and three yards to go. You are the running back. The play has been called for you to receive the ball and run left. You know if you don't make the three yards and get a first down, the game is essentially over.

The ball is hiked. The quarterback turns and hands you the ball. You start running as hard and as fast as you can. It is your training coupled with your deep inner 'Dream" which propels your run. It is your faith which assures you that you <u>can</u> and <u>will</u> make it.

Self confidence is your agreement with yourself based on your recollection of your experiences in similar situations.

Faith is your agreement with trusted relationships with your God and all others who share your beliefs, not only in similar situations, but also in different unexpected ones as well.

~ ~ ~

"HUMOR"

The comedy of relaxing our seriousness and acknowledging – we've fouled up again.

Granddaddy's Mules

It's amazing how accustomed we get to the tools we use. And how often is it when we use a convenient tool rather than one perhaps better suited for the job at hand. I am reminded of my granddaddy plowing his garden for a couple of rows of tomatoes. Accustomed as he was to using the double mule team for plowing, it was probably a bit of an over-kill for the tomato rows. I can still see the scene - and hear both him and Grandma yelling at each other while the mules drooled from their inner laughter.

Sweaty reins draped over his shoulders, he grabbed onto both handles of the plow, like it was a life and death situation, yelling instructions to the mules, often cursing them when they didn't listen, which was as usual. He only used the reins when all else failed. Like when they stepped too far to the left and wiped out an entire row of cabbages. They felt the reins then…and a few choice words. He never would plow on Sunday. When he finished, he had two rows for tomatoes, a lot of future mulch, and little left in the day.

We know how he felt, don't we?

For example, just the other morning when I looked up to glance at my mule team, as I was attempting to simply convert one type of computer file to a web-supported JPG format, I noticed that the mules weren't there. Instead, I was driving a very powerful computer program called Photoshop, which works like a computerized 747 jet airplane, with all four engines running at full speed. Just as I was thinking about the cabbage row, the plane veered to the left and wiped out two barns, the pickup truck and the top of the chimney.

But by early afternoon, it was finally done. Now, remembering the mules again, I thought to myself, if I can get this 747 started again, I think I will fly upstairs and get some lunch.

~ ~ ~

A Sunday in April

Preface: In our mother's later years she lived at an assisted living facility, and the four of us children and our spouses helped take care of her. One of the activities that Kate and I always enjoyed was taking Mom to church each Sunday. Betty Jean and Pat, my two sisters, would visit Mom during the week and on Friday. During that visit, they would select and tag a dress in Mom's closet for her to wear on Sunday. When, Kate and I arrived, Mom was usually dressed and ready to go. After each of our times with Mom, we would then send an e-mail to the rest of us, updating us on how things went. Here is an e-mail I sent back in April, 2001.

Today was one of those Sundays. Aside from the off-on rain and the gloomy half-lit clouds, several things happened today to set it w-a-y apart from our usual pleasant Sundays. No one was hurt. But we had some difficult afternoon times. It started off fairly normal. Mom was aware of her tagged dress in the bedroom closet when I talked with her on the telephone this morning. We left a little early just in case.

As we approached the back entrance gates to the Plaza to pick up Mom, I slowed the car down to ease over the dip in the road – right at the gates. BJ and Pat, you know that depression in the pavement that I am talking about, which is a part of the road drainage. Today, for some reason, I glanced over at the repaired steel gate on the right side and noticed the freshly painted black members, which hopefully would never be closed again, at least during daylight hours. Little did I know that later I would have another very close and long look at that right black gate.

We picked up Mom, and on our way out of the gates, we moved slowly again over the dip in the road. As we did, we saw an old dirty-red 1985 ford pickup truck, piled high with firewood, heading towards the Plaza – and the gates. I wondered if the aging unshaven driver knew about the dip in the road. As we passed each other on the road, I glanced in the rear-view mirror and soon saw that he didn't. He hit the dip at almost full speed and -- chunk, clank, s-c-r-a-t-c-h, and he added his own set of bumper and frame skid marks on the pavement along with those of other unsuspecting drivers, like first-time church bus drivers, whose passengers often bounced aloft in Bush Gardens fashion -- some being crowned good as they hit the ceiling hard.

But the old pickup truck had it even worse. Overloaded anyway, rear tires nearly flat with the heavy logs, the truck bounced way up and threw most of the top layer of logs high over the truck and then all over the road. I shook my head in disbelief and sorrow for the poor guy as we rounded the curve towards Hermitage Road on our way to church and our timed appointment with the church parking lot. I lost sight of the calamity and wondered why in the world a spring delivery of firewood was going to the Plaza? What is management up to now? Thank goodness we were not in the truck's path back at the gates. But the worse is yet to come.

Church and lunch were fine, as usual. Scott and his three little ones joined us. On our way out of the Dilly, we were caught in one of those sudden downpours, and we had to hustle to get to the car. Kate and Mom got in quickly, I closed Mom's door and dashed around to my door hurriedly. As I did, I noticed out of the corner of my eye that part of Mom's skirt was still hanging out of the door. By the time that I realized what I had seen, I was jumping in the car on my side. "Should I go back in the heavy rain, or wait a minute or two? Will Mom's skirt get wet?" I wondered.

I decided to drive off slowly as I thought about it further. And just as soon as the shower caught us, it essentially stopped. Then, one of those tail-gaters started pressuring me to move on. So I did, thinking that Mom's skirt is certainly okay now. It stopped raining for the moment, and since we would be at the Plaza in a few minutes, everything would be just fine. So I thought. We drove on the Plaza – with Mom's skirt partially hanging out of the tightly closed door.

When we approached the Plaza back gates, I couldn't believe what I saw. There were at least a dozen of round logs still laying in the dip in the road – some parallel to the dip, some across it. The old guy apparently just left them there. Most of them were small and easy enough to grab and toss back into the truck – that lazy, z%%#2!!

After saying a few other choice words to myself, I decided to proceed on across the logs, instead of going through the exit gate next to us. That was a mistake. As we started across the small logs, the front wheels made it fine. But the back wheels climbed up on some of the round logs, and they started to roll. Then the whole car started shifting to the right. "Oh no," I thought. "I could see it happening." We rolled slowly but steadily, directly into that right gate – and finally stopped hard up against those same freshly painted hard steel bars. As Mom looked out of her window, all she could see was black bars. I didn't hear a crunch, so hopefully I didn't dent the door. It started to rain again. I turned on the emergency blinkers, got the umbrella out of the trunk and walked around to the right side. We were wedged hard up against the gate, yet fortunately there were no dents that I could see. Kate was shaking her head, the same way Mom did when I fell into the tadpole creek. Somehow, getting wet seems to bring more clouds near me.

But this called for careful analysis. Within seconds I realized that if I tried to move the car, still perched on logs like a roller derby, I would surely scrape the side of the car very badly. "What I need," I thought to myself, "is a wrecker truck to pull the car to the left and then forward (or backward) so that I could get off of the logs." So, I told Mom and Kate that I was going to call for a wrecker, and that we would be out of this mess shortly. In the meantime, I would walk them to Mom's building under the umbrella, and they could wait there. Okay, they agreed. But both would have to get out of the car on my side.

"Hey, my skirt is caught in the door," Mom said.

"Oh yeah," I said to myself, now remembering. "Now what?" We tried opening the door, with me outside under the umbrella, and Mom inside, but it wouldn't budge more than an 1/8 of an inch – not quite enough. Mom's skirt was apparently caught over the bottom hem, which was a good thick one. I went around and got in the back seat to pull harder. There I was leaning over Mom pulling her skirt against the door, emergency blinkers still flashing, and passers-by wondering what in the world is going on here? I could picture me ripping the skirt, so I eased up. Need to think this out, I said to myself. But, then it just got worse.

"I really have to go to the bathroom," Mom said.

I just laughed. This now was really getting funny. Now what? I remembered what BJ and Pat had told me about the urgency when Mom needed to go to the bathroom. We probably didn't have time to wait for the wrecker, which I hadn't called yet.

We sat there for a minute or two, Kate and I looking at each other, between the swings of her head, back and forth. "Any suggestions?" I asked. We discussed some options.

"Okay, this is the best we can come up with," I said. "Mom will have to get out of her skirt. She can wear my slacks, which I will remove in the car, and Mom can put them on temporarily. Then Mom and Kate can walk to the Plaza (and the bathroom) under the umbrella, while I wait here in the car. Mom can wait in her apartment, change into another skirt, Kate can bring my pants back, I will put them back on, call a wrecker, and we will be on our way."

There was a long pause. Moments later, I was sitting in the car, alone in the driver's seat in my underwear bottoms, and Kate was walking with Mom, under the umbrella, parachuted in my Sunday slacks gathered multiple times around Mom's waste. I started to laugh with them, but -- then, I saw red flashing lights. "Oh no!!" I sighed…as a police car pulled up, apparently called by one of the suspecting neighbors. "What am I going to say? Even worse, when I looked into the police car -- it was a police LADY. Suppose she asks me to get out of the car?"

Hey, this could go on and on – until it is finally resolved. But now it's probably time to remind you that this Sunday was April 1st. So, I got you three again. APRIL FOOL!

Fortunately, all of this happened in our imagination. Today was great after all, in spite of the rain. This love-based April Fool joke was inspired by my little sister, BJ, in her Friday e-mail, where she told me to be careful this Sunday, because it's April Fool. Thanks BJ. Hope this brought a bit of joy and humor for your day.

Mom is fine. All is well. We had a wonderful Sunday.
Love to all.

~ ~ ~

Sunday at Cape Canaveral

Now, in closing this Chapter, I have a true story of a happening another Sunday with Mom and family at a local restaurant. Kate and I were with Mom after church, then our son Scott and his family joined us. We were all sitting down, just getting ready to eat when I reached for my yet unopened straw. I could already see a twinkle in Mom's eyes.

You see I have this standing joke with all of my grandchildren -- whenever I prepare to use a straw, I carefully remove an end of the paper covering, then twist the other end to prepare it ready to shoot the covering off (gently) at one of the grandchildren. It's just one of the ways I can be a child again and tell them in their own language that I love them.

Today, I selected Miss Holly, age 6, who was sitting about eight feet away, and already grinning at what was about to happen. I aimed and very gently blew into the straw missile, hoping that it would stop just short of her plate. Instead, it sailed by her, climbing in altitude as if powered by some magic engine. It kept sailing across the dining room – then landed in an elderly lady's upper part of her white puffy hairdo.

The landing was of such grace and precision that she never felt or saw it maneuver into its parking space. I waited to catch her eye so I could apologize for what my grandson had done sitting next to me. But she never looked up. She just kept eating. What was I to do? If I went over to her now, surely it would be more of an embarrassment to her. Certainly, her elderly husband, sitting directly across from the now feathered hairdo, would see it and remove it, and then look around for an apology. I could address it then…but, he just kept on eating. That parked missile went on for the ride, bobbing up and down with each new lunch bite.

Our entire table was now in hysterics. At one time, the husband seemed to notice it, and I thought this would all be over. But no. If he saw it, he probably thought it was part of a new style his wife was trying -- and he wasn't about to simply yank it off. So they just kept on eating. And our table, including Mom, vibrated with giggles and embarrassments. Finally, they started getting ready to stand up. They did stand up, with her sprouting her new needle-like white paper bonnet. Then, he noticed the funny ornament. And off it was whisked as they both walled away. Whew! Next time, I will have to aim a bit lower.

~ ~ ~

Why this word HUMOR is important

A person without a sense of humor is like a wagon without springs. It's jolted by every pebble on the road.
Henry Ward Beecher

Common sense and sense of humor is the same thing, moving at different speeds. A sense of humor is just common sense dancing.
William James

Humor is mankind's greatest blessing.
Mark Twain

Sometimes it's very difficult to think or appreciate humor, isn't it? But still, with practice, I try not to leave home without it.

~ ~ ~

8 - THE EIGHTH WORD

"HEALTH"

Preface: This word is obviously important. Here are two examples to help illustrate that. The first is a poem of a terrible incurable disease over which victims have little control over its attack or progress. The second is one in which we do have some control over both its probability and progress. Both examples are pleas to do what you can to help yourself and others.

Multiple Sclerosis

Imagine -- we grasp hands,

extend our reach tip to tip to tip,

and stretch wide together, all of us,

to encircle this ravaging storm,

squeeze its eye, its seed of destruction,

and lay open its hidden secrets.

And with our minds then focused,

we dissect this whirling monster,

which rips apart human systems,

uproots the forests of our souls,

erodes embankments of hope,

and overlays its veil of misery.

Do you feel the touch of fingertips,

to confront this Mighty Storm,

with vigor, resources and love,

to unwind this twisted invader,

this MS category 8 tempest,

which leaves but wailing silence,

and cold dry rain?

~ ~ ~

A Message to the Captain

Heart surgery is a traumatic experience. Anesthetized nightmares, wild illusions and constant wallops of deep seated pain rock the soul. About 24 hours after my triple bypass operation, I also began having strange feelings about an imminent urgency for someone I cared about.

However, I couldn't identify the particular individual. I just sensed that someone needed warning of possible serious danger, quickly. I felt the impending peril so strongly, that three days later, when I left the hospital and returned home, I found myself, still wracked with the pain of recovery, sitting at my computer and recording, the best as I could remember, this story -- for someone I must reach as soon as possible.

Would you consider for a moment that part of this someone might be...you, or someone you know?

I see you first witnessing the death of a huge crippled pleasure ship, as your own cruise ship almost one-half mile away, waits by in rescue. As you lean over the cold steel rail just outside of your service quarters, you see the enormous ship gasp its last surge for survival. Then there is a violent explosion in its engine room.

You see pieces of the engine, parts you would recognize anywhere, tumbling high in the air. Then another explosion blasts huge fiery holes through the hull. Moments later, among the screams of horror and shock, you see the arrogant mass -- tons of glimmering slabs of steel, tilt its bow steeply towards the heavens, as if in a final plea for amnesty. Then silhouetted against the endless horizon, it slips slowly into the depths of a watery grave. You are jolted by those sights, the yells of those displaced, and the smell of burning fuel, its heat flushing your face even at nearly a half mile away.

Soon, terrified and exhausted survivors begin boarding your ship. You meet several colleagues who had your same duty assignment on the lost ship. This is unusual, because most service personnel in your line of work usually get caught in the middle of such disasters and are severely injured, or even go down with the ship.

Later, you shudder at what you learn might have caused the disaster. Communications throughout the doomed ship and to the Captain were severely hampered. Messages to and from the officers' bridge were oriented primarily around the pleasures of the passengers, apparently even at the sacrifice of their safety. You shudder; that's the way it is here, on your ship, too.

You move through the service decks below, and see the work teams dressed according to their responsibilities. Your unit, the HDL crew has the primary responsibility to keep all of the corridors and main pipe lines clear. You've often wondered what the HDL signifies, and if it has any connection with HDL cholesterol that you've heard about. That is interesting, because here, your assignment also follows just behind the work of the LDL crew. LDL is another type of cholesterol, often called the bad guys. Here on ship, the LDL crew could be called that as well, because, while providing their own operating functions, they also often leave endless trails of trash and damages to the corridor walls and sometimes crushed or damaged pipes.

Some of the rescued service staff from the lost ship confirm more of your own apprehensions about the safety of the ship. You learn that a certain number of HDL guys are required to keep up with the LDL guys and maintain the circulation routes. If the LDL crew greatly exceeds the proportionate balance of HDL workers, you simply can't keep pace. Clutter abounds, clogging begins, damages go unattended, and pipes weaken and rupture.

Delivery of fuel and coolant to the main engine is delayed, the engine overheats and eventually a lock-up or explosion is highly possible. Phase one of this has already happened, as you have detected numerous piping problems.

You don't know who or what actually determines the number of HDL and LDL workers. But, you have some clues. You remember those times during practice maneuvers without passengers, when the ship was driven hard for thirty minutes or so. The number of LDL guys really appeared to thin out.

You also remember when the ship stopped at certain ports and filled up with greasy looking fuel oil. The LDL guys came out in droves, as if nurtured by the hovering fumes heavy laden with deposits they seem to enjoy. This was brought to the attention of the Captain. But, the Captain ignored such warnings -- and continues still to hear only what supports the passenger's fantasies, as if all is well.

Then, later it begins to happen. As the ship pulls into port, you hear the engine, its gigantic piston pumping hard -- struggling. You hear the ship's horn shouting as if to say -- "we have arrived." You hear bands playing on shore, welcoming the eager spenders. And, there are the cheers of passengers applauding new adventures and excitement. You think to yourself -- thank God, we made it to another port.

You walk out on the service deck and gaze at the lush island port beyond, another temporary paradise, the symbol of what this cruise represents for many. You lean over the rail looking up above, and you see the Captain, grinning and waving to the crowd and the cheering passengers. Then, your knees buckle as your eyes make contact with the Captain's. A shock vibrates down your spine. It's impossible! Yet, there it is. The Captain's face. It is YOUR face. You, or another part of you -- are the Captain. The Captain looks down at you, winks and smiles again.

Bewildered, you look around and behind you, as if trying to confirm that you are really here. Then, you look back up at the Captain, still playing to the crowd. What is this?

You see your Captain waving and casting broad grins to everyone. Then there's a sudden grimace. The Captain grabs tightly at the bridge railing -- then clutches at the bright white uniform, reaching for the chest through the spotless brass-buttoned coat. You feel a flutter inside your chest. The Captain staggers and slumps to the deck as the cheers quickly turn to silence, and then "Ohhh no's". You start to shout from your service deck below..

"It's the Captain's heart! Get help! It's his heart!"

But, your words go unheard, again -- like you're in another room, separated by a glass partition. Then, you hear some rumblings down from the engine room. A gush of white steam blows through the service door. You can hear the engine struggling harder. You know what is about to happen -- you yell up at the bridge again.

"May Day! Get help...Now! May Day!"

But, it's like screaming into a vacuum. No one hears you. Then, you can't get your words out. You try to speak again, but there's no breath – then you slowly drop to the deck and lose consciousness.

Later, you hear the voice of the Captain again, this time muffled as though under water. We're sunk. You knew it would eventually happen. But, you learn instead that the Captain has recovered and is generally okay. His booming voice is now resonating through nearby pipes -- new pipes which the ship had added with other extensive repairs. Now, it is preparing to return to duty.

The Captain's voice carries with it a new sense of urgency, a fresh resolute, yet calm command -- one that you seldom heard before. You discover through the Captain's requests to the ship's officers, a new and different awareness of all of the service staff throughout the ship. There appears to be a new desire from the Captain to seek messages from everyone. But, you wonder, will it prevail? Will it make any difference?

You look for some answers to these questions during a practice run around a couple of the island ports. No passengers. But the entire crew is on board with new engine piping -- and much anticipation. During the rehearsal, the ship is driven hard during thirty minute intervals. The stiff breeze blowing against your face, pulls wind-tears from the corners of your eyes, and reminds you of the cleansing effects of rigorous exertion -- and maybe recent experiences.

Later, the ship is refueled -- with clear sparkling oil, the very best. Port officials board the ship and log the number of LDL and HDL crew, and soon usher several LDL crew members off ship, maintaining a prescribed ratio of crew. This has never happened before.

Then during the run back to home port, the Captain issues the command for the last new practice routine.

"This will be performed once a day," the Captain clamors, "every day, without fail."

The ship's bells sound a new ring. The huge steam horn blasts two short bursts, and the ship immediately coasts to a gradual stop. All systems are shut down. And, the ship just drifts quietly. No sounds or movements by the crew. You notice a strange enhanced awareness of the wholeness of the ship. Still no audible exchanges, but the staff senses each other's presence. The prolonged quiet draws out silent thoughts of "So what now?"

Then, "So what?" Then, mostly just quiet. A restorative peaceful calm slowly breathes within. After a few more moments, the shut-down ends, and actions slowly begin again.

As the ship pulls into home port, you realize that the silence routine will be a real problem for many of the passengers. And, you wonder how the Captain will handle that. Just as this thought passes through your mind, you are handed an official notice offering you the opportunity to be transferred to another ship, where activities and procedures will be closer to what you are accustomed. You are advised to respond immediately to the Captain in person, or it will be assumed that you accept the transfer.

You stare at the notice bewildered. Then, you fold it, put it in your pocket, and ponder your next step. Another ship would mean very few changes. But here, serving the Captain's revisions would require many modifications. Some will surely generate failures. Overtime will be required. And, you know that most of the passengers will continue to howl for constant entertainment and thrills. Yes, this next cruise will be a real dilly. Another ship would be a breeze.

You also know that the Captain will still push to reach each port exactly on time, as before. But -- still, there's something different now. There appears to be a new focus on the process of getting there, rather than just the destination alone. You wonder if you might find some benefits in the Captain's new plan -- even beyond the higher probability of the ship's longer-term survival.

Suddenly, the Captain appears above, fresh, in full white uniform with those sparkling brass buttons jingling with new protocol. The Captain looks you straight in the eyes -- and you see yourself again, looking back at another part of yourself, as if dissipated among thousands of other segments of you, each with internal whispers and nudges, all grasping for meaning.

"Do you wish to serve with us?" The Captain asked.

You roll your thoughts and mixed feelings in your mind. You remember the exploding lost ship. You think about all of the changes that have to be made here. You wonder. You try to assemble an answer from your confusion.

"Well, come on!" The Captain wailed. "Which will it be? Yes or no?"

Moments later, you feel your head slowly and instinctively motioning, confirming your message to the Captain. And while the signal is a bit frail, it is "loud and clear" to both of you.

~ ~ ~

Why this word HEALTH is important

Because it plays a major role in how many years we may practice all of the other 11 words. Imagine yourself as being the Capitan and your body as the ship. Maybe you are in perfect health and shape. Most of us aren't. Are we going to hear those unusual moans down in the engine room? Are our pipes reasonable clear? I hope you never forget this word, Health, and I hope this story may help remind you. Best wishes, Captain.

9 - THE NINETH WORD

"OTHERS"

We share our space in time and place with family, friends, and all others.

Friends

One Sunday years ago, I witnessed TWO great sermons...just minutes apart. After church, while I was waiting for Mom and Kate in the hall outside of the restrooms, something happened alongside the dozens of people rushing to their cars. Across the hall, sitting in a row of chairs along the walls were several members of our deaf church. They were signing and signaling each other joyfully as they always do after church -- except one nicely dressed elderly black lady, who sat there motionless with a somber stare through her dark sun glasses. She was apparently also blind and alone in a dark silent world, in the middle of a busy hallway route.

Then, down the hall walked another deaf member, a younger man. He walked slowly up to the blind lady, and then painstakingly kneeled down in front of her so that his arms, face and hands were at the same level as hers. Next, he picked up her hands and placed his signing hands inside her palms and began communicating with her. He took her hands and placed them on his partially bearded face so she would know who he was, and she began beaming with joy. Her head nodded in acknowledgment of her friend. She smiled over and over, as they shared thoughts between hands. She laughed in her silent way, head still nodding up and down ... as he exchanged his fellowship and care with her.

Others, walking busily down the hall entirely missed this beautiful sermon. But a few of us, accidentally at the right place at the right time, became captivated by this demonstration of great human love for a friend. One could feel it radiating between and from these two. They continued to share their joy, and slowly I became captured by another participant in the communication. It was the glow of God's presence, shining from the heart of that kneeling friend, showing the rest of us how to really serve. There must have been a similar glow when Jesus knelt before his disciples to wash their feet. I felt my grin widen in awe and reached up to wiggle off another tear. Then, I felt ashamed that I needed to be reminded again that we see God's love in our love for others. And, I almost missed it again.

~ ~ ~

Grandma's Biscuits

Preface: Starting when I was about 14, I spent part of my summers at my Grandfather's and Grandmother's farm near Chase City, Virginia. I helped feed the hogs, gather eggs from the chickens, weed the garden, work in the tobacco fields, and help harvest the tobacco. One summer I painted the side porch where Grandma and I used to sit on each evening – and talk. All of the meals Grandma prepared were from home grown foods, even the flour was ground from wheat grown on the farm. Each morning about 5 am, Granddaddy would get up and start a fire in the wood cook stove. Then, about the time Grandma got up around 6 am, it was good and hot -- ready for her biscuits and the rest of her wonderful breakfast. Her biscuits were one of her trademarks. Here are a few recollections about those magnificent biscuits.

My grandmother had the unique ability to "size-up" strangers by the way they ate her biscuits. She didn't intentionally do that.

It just happened automatically as they digested those delicious tools of human expression. I could tell that a session was about to begin, when she brought a plate of the hot steaming biscuits to the coffee table...right in front of a visiting encyclopedia salesman, or a new neighbor. They never knew what hit them.

She watched the way they ate and how they talked -- like a computerized hawk. She observed how they spread the home-churned butter, how they held the soft flaky biscuits, and how large a bite they took with each gulp. These were important signals to her. Then, she listened. A muffled reaction like, "These are just wonderful..." meant one thing. "Did you make these from an old recipe?" meant something else. And, "Is this local flour?" usually signified a short visit.

She didn't appreciate people trying to analyze her biscuits, or her family. "Educated fools," she would say. "They're so busy trying to figure out why my biscuits are good -- that they never get around to enjoying them."

Maybe that was one of the reasons she married my grandfather. He never talked when he ate her biscuits. He would just sit quietly and pour a little sorghum molasses on his plate, right next to a treasured clump of butter. Then he would stir the two together with his knife and the edge of a warm biscuit. Stirring was important. There must have been several chemical reactions occurring there on the plate. I saw another one. My grandmother watching out of the corner of her eye, as my grandfather raised to his mouth his prized collection of ingredients riding on the biscuit. I think what really got to my grandmother was the way he closed his eyes and smiled, faintly but quite naturally, as he ingested each cherished mouthful. Two examples of pure love at its best. My grandfather eating biscuits, and my grandmother watching. No one could eat biscuits like my grandfather.

As I reflect on those biscuit moments, I wonder how we might stand up to her tests today. I wonder too about how she really did it. Thinking back, I believe she looked for two reactions.

One was the intellectualized or "educated fool" response. I think she saw here the biscuit taster relying on artificial criteria to help evaluate his or her reaction -- perhaps because they did not yet trust their own personal judgment. They responded to the ingredients of the biscuits rather than to the biscuits themselves. Maybe saying something like, "Hmmmm, these appear to contain vegetable shortening rather than animal fat. Is that correct?" Or, "Do I detect a bit of sugar in here?" Grandma would just sit, echoing a blank look across her face.

Another part of this academic response that got her goat was the "history connection," as she called it. The ingredients served as the synthetic focus again, but this time they were analyzed from a historical standpoint. I can hear her now mimicking one of her favorites. "These ingredients appear to be typical of early American Southern breads popularized by home cooking, then later incorporated by restaurants nationwide."

To Grandma, these people were missing much of what was happening, in their lives...and certainly what was happening in her biscuits. To her, they missed the whole point -- enjoying the biscuits. They probably weren't enjoying life either. She would often reply to their over-intellectualized questions with one of her own. "Not allergic to rat-flour, are ya?"

"I've never seen taste buds wake up so fast," she chuckled as she revealed some of her pranks to me one evening...just after the sudden departure of an encyclopedia salesman.

But Grandma found a true friend when a guest really enjoyed the savory taste of her biscuits. When she heard something like, "These are just wonderful,"...she knew she had met a new pal, one with the right values in life. She didn't explain much about this type of reaction, but I gathered from the glow spreading across her face that this signified the second type of response she was looking for, more of a sensorial response compared with an intellectualized one. I believe it was Grandma's way of acknowledging the purity of what we call today, "present moments."

~ ~ ~

Signals at Easter

Pete can't believe what he is seeing. After all, it is Easter Sunday, and people are already arriving at church dressed to the hilt in fresh spring outfits. Flowers are everywhere. The choir is adorned in special Easter robes. Yet, walking up the aisle from the side entrance is a scruffy unshaven man, inappropriately dressed in bags of wrinkles.

"What is he trying to do here," Pete asks himself? "This man must know what a scene he is causing. I've never seen him here before. He must have gotten by the ushers. Why didn't he wait until next week when so many of today's special guests wouldn't be here?"

No sooner than those thoughts formed, the man walked up the aisle to Pete's row, turned, and sat down in a vacant seat right next to him. Pete couldn't believe what was happening. He could feel the eyes of everyone around him, staring at him. He wonders, "Suppose they think this guy is a friend of mine?" As a Christian, he realizes that his objective is to love and accept all others as God's children. And he has, in most instances.

But, just as Pete reminds himself of that, his nose confirms the laundry history of this man's garments. No doubt, so does everyone else around him. Whew! It is difficult for Pete to sing with such a frown on his face. But he manages, not wanting to draw any more attention to this most embarrassing situation.

The man sits quietly throughout the service. At the conclusion, the minister requests, as he often does, for members to greet guests sitting nearby – and welcome them back. Pete acknowledges those normal steps to himself, but those gestures seem perfect to make sure everyone around him understands this man is no acquaintance of his.

So, as the service ends, Pete turns towards the man and timidly extends his right hand to beckon a quick handshake and said, "First time here, right?" The man looks at Pete. When their eyes meet, Pete feels a deep loving sorrow looking back at him, almost through him -- a staring glistening glow, as the man whispered, "Is this your house of prayer?"

Pete is captivated by the question and doesn't notice the man's left arm reach up and rest on Pete's shoulder as he waits for an answer. Nor did Pete see what the others behind him can now plainly see. But Pete could feel the man's right hand, now accepting his extended handshake, as the stranger inclines his head emphasizing his waiting question -- while pressing a deep palm scar into Pete's denying clasp.

And a rooster signaled anew
yet again -- cock-a-doodle-do.

Like Peter's doubts, three befores,
smeared deep with pain and sores,
now this man too, belongs to you,
and you and you -- and yes to you.

Deny still, God, our actions true,
forgive us, Lord, way beyond fours

for yes, surely this man is You,
and like us all, he too is Yours.

Today is one of joy and peace,
away with exclusions and pride.
Today we pray illusions cease
and outpourings of love abide.

Today we celebrate victory.
Today Your love wins once again.
Praise to Your divine mastery,
Which signals our heart. Amen.

~ ~ ~

When I Was Your Age

To the "old" girls and guys (like me): When we were growing up, how often did we hear our elders proclaim, "When I was your age..." then they would follow with a course of action that they took which was very different than what we were already taking. Their implied course of action, of course, was completely irrelevant to the situation at hand. Remember those times, "old" girls and guys? Well, now we're doing the same thing to our youngsters, right? Hold on for a moment. I'll be right back.

Now, to the "young" girls and guys: Wouldn't you have liked to be there then – maybe just as a squirrel on a nearby tree, or as a fly on the wall, to listen in when your elder folks at a young age had to face that same snobbish unfair comparison "When I was your age?" Wouldn't it be fun to find out the real truth – how they really felt at your age, what they really did at your age?

Well, now through the magic of time-shifts and a dialog format in this piece between the young and old, between what old agers might think is happening and what really is happening to the young agers.

You see, now I am old but still have a steel memory of so many major foul-ups that happened to me over 70 years ago, and what my elders suggested I do about them, plus what I actually did – it may be revealing for all four of us to move through one of these true foul-ups together. Four of us means you "old" readers, you "young" readers, plus the "old" me (OM) (the ghost writer) and the "young" me (YM) the true story teller.

Most of the writing in this piece will be done by OM, and it will be in this regular format. When the YM butts in, I mean contributes to the writing, *his format will be in italics.*

When I was just over three years old we moved into a nice small frame house on Patterson Avenue in Richmond, Virginia. It was built and owned by the family next door, the Tylers. There were actually two generations of Tylers next door, and all of them were very nice people. There were Granddaddy and Grandmother, Dad and Mom, plus two sons and a daughter. Most of my dealings were with Granddaddy Tyler who had a lot of time to spend with me – explaining things, especially about the outdoor goldfish pond he had built.

One day after we settled in and I was around four years old, my uncle Gordon came to visit us. He and I palled around a lot too. *Yeah, I liked him because he answered a lot of my questions and never really told me what to do.* One sunny and warm day we went for a walk towards the school about a half block away. *Seemed more like three blocks to me and my short legs.* When we got to the corner, we stopped at the wooded lot there and just looked around. *Yeah, I was tired as ever, plus I had what you folks now call a wedgie. I wanted to stay a while so I started looking down at the leaves and stuff on the ground. I spotted something and picked it up.*

Gordon noticed that I had picked up an old pack of matches, with several of them still unused. Gordon started to get a little upset over me holding the matches. *Yeah, because I asked him what they were.* Gordon said, "They're matches, give them to me, okay?" *Nothing doing. I need more information. I asked him what they're for.* Gordon said, "They're dangerous, so you should let me hold them, for you. *Dangerous, I think I have heard that word before, but I've never seen a pack of dangerous like this. So I asked him, "How do you use dangerous?"* Gordon took the matches. *I thought he was different. I asked him again, "How do you use dangerous?"*

"They're matches," he said, "and I use them to light cigarettes.." as he pulled one match from the pack and dragged it along the edge of the pack. It flared up and he accidentally dropped it to the ground. Some of the leaves caught fire, but he quickly stomped them out. *Oh, I see now how to use dangerous, so as he was stomping I took the pack and pulled a couple of them from the pack and dragged them like he did along the edge. There was a big hot flash that started to burn me, so I threw the pack away from me (and Gordon).*

The pack sort of bounced and started two small fires. Gordon rushed to them and began stomping as fast as he could, exclaiming, "Why did you do that? Looks at the fires you started. When I was your age, I never did anything like this. This is bad." *I did that because you just taught me to do that. Yeah, I see the fires. They're pretty and getting bigger."* "Help me out here!!" Gordon yelled. "This is getting worse. HELP!!"

How can I help? I can't dance like that, except when I was only 1 year old and my diaper was really full for a long time. I wondered if he had a diaper on now. I was just thinking without talking, I didn't have time to really ask him. He was acting like something was wrong here. Never seen him like this. What's that sound?

A neighbor had called the fire department. *Hey, this is even better. Look at that neat red truck, and the man wearing a raincoat – carrying a funny long bucket with a hose on it.* "Thank God you're here," Gordon said, "We've had a little accident." *I don't know what accident meant. I thought we were having a little dangerous.*

The nice fireman shot the fire with his hose and the fire disappeared. *Gordon and the man in the raincoat stopped all of the fun. Looks like Gordon is sad...don't' know why. Wonder what he's thinking.*

Yeah, I'm thinking alright (Gordon) ....one of these days, kid, when you are my age, I'm going to tell your children what you did when you were their age. Talk about dangerous. Ha!

~ ~ ~

Sausage and Egg Biscuit

Kate and I had lots of memories about Mom and Dad too, during Thanksgiving. Ours started with breakfast. We decided to go to church for the 10am service, and we would follow our normal Sunday routine, which began with breakfast at McDonald's (fairly low-fat w/good protein Egg-McMuffin and coffee). Turned out, however, that the McDonald's on West Patterson, as well as its Burger King neighbor, were both closed. So we drove on closer to church with our nose sniffing the air for a slight departure from the fall air. The time remaining would not allow for a "real" departure, like Bob Evans, so we scanned the fast food options along the way. After seeing that the Burger King at Patterson and Parham was also closed, we decided to turn north on Parham and see what turned up. Up ahead, bustling

under its normal cloud of grille smoke and cars was Hardee's --
special caterer of memory lane.

For it was just a few dozen years ago when all packed for
Myrtle Beach, the six of us plus Mom and Dad, all in one car,
knew what crossing the Carolina line meant. It was time for
breakfast! After a lengthy discussion, Dad said that Hardees has
the best sausage and egg biscuits of all. The driver agreed. As
we pulled in the parking lot Mom was still reviewing why Dad
should NOT know who has the best sausage and egg biscuits.
But the aroma overcame all of us, and we walked in smiling as if
we had already eaten. Yes, they WERE the best sausage and egg
biscuits, again.

Thanksgiving morning, Kate and I had another one...and they
still are. Most of our Thanksgiving breakfast conversation was
about Mom and Dad, and how thankful we are for their love and
sharing. Later, the minister reminded us whenever we are in
difficult times, that being thankful is like an antibiotic. Loving
thankfulness and depression cannot sit at the same table.

Thank all of you out there for your presence in our families.
Your love and smiles continue to be the sausage and egg biscuits
for our soul, which we will never forget.

~ ~ ~

Rapid Eye Movement

REM -- the signal
of dreams in bloom,
communed in vivid colors
painted deep by our spirits.

REM – the escort
to New York each night
in darts among bent steel
arm in arm with 3,500 silences,

who hover yet in peace
while their brief message
connects us again
in REMs of tomorrow.

~ ~ ~

Where Two or Three are Gathered Together

As noted elsewhere among these 12 Words, during the sunset years of my mother's life, she lived at an assisted living facility in Richmond. My wife Kate and I would pick Mom up each Sunday morning and take her to church.

On our way to church, Mom would so often tell Kate and me of the joys she had that week playing her piano in the dining room for the residents. They all would sing hymns together. Often they would continue singing through dessert and into the cleanup phase and beyond. Mom so loved that time, and her resident friends loved it too. It was one of Mom's greatest ministries; inspiring others with her music. Often as Kate and I walked down Mom's hallways to our car, residents would stop Mom, look into her eyes and ask if she would be playing the piano tonight. Mom always answered, "Yes, God willing." There was a very special relationship there among her resident friends.

During the Christmas season of 1999; my two sisters along with my brother came up with a great idea to host a special sing-along gathering at Mom's place for her and her resident friends, staff and outside guests. Mom, my two sisters, a cousin could play the piano during the sing along. It was to be a very special music event to be held just after the Christmas season. Weeks before the event, I wondered what I could do to help. I immediately knew that one way to help was for me NOT to sing. My brother and sisters agreed.

But maybe I could help Mom another way. As I searched some of Mom's favorite Bible verses, I came across Matthew 18. And that's where I found the words I was looking for. And the context in the verses was relationships. That's certainly what my Mom was doing through her music – nurturing relationships. Well so, how could I bring this all together for the upcoming concert to support Mom and maybe even add to her ministry?

Later, an idea came to me to develop new lyrics for one of Mom's favorite hymns – words which would connect parts of Matthew 18 and what Mom and her friends were doing. Mom and I talked about it. Then she and I made a list of her favorite hymns. I went through those and picked "What a Friend We Have in Jesus." The tune was so familiar to many people and it could be sung from memory.

So, I began composing new hymn lyrics, springing from Matthew 18. That 20th verse says exactly what I saw happening at Mom's dinner hymn sings. "For where two of three are gathered together in my name, there am I in the midst of them."

As I began writing, I imagined – what Mom may have been thinking as a wish-message to those in the dining room. I think it was, "Come join in." So, that became the message of the first stanza.

1 - Come and join us all to sing now,
Help our spirits chase the gloom,
Sweep away our cares with praises,
And our joys will fill this room.

And the chorus then tells us why.

Chorus:
For where two or three are gathered,
Together in His name,
He is in the midst among them,
Filling hearts with love's proclaim.

The second wish-message I sensed was, "We are all one big family here." So that thought became the 2nd stanza.

2 - We are all like one big family,
Leaning on each other's days,
With a Precious time to offer,
All our voices to God's praise.

The third wish-message became, "Let's celebrate His presence."

3 - Celebrate His presence here now;
See that smile across my face.
Yes, the grin is deep from within,
flowing from His loving Grace.

Well, Mom played that hymn during that special sing-along event – while about 50 or so sang the words with her. She also played it many times at her dinner concerts – up until her death.

Then, I thought these new lyrics would surely retire too, as her theme-song to gather her friends together and sing praises to God. And, as far as I know, the words were silent for many years.

Then, I received my sister, Pat's e-mail asking me about the possibility of using the first stanza and chorus of Mom's hymn as the choral introit for worship services in her church. Several Sundays later I was asked to speak at the worship service relating to the congregation how the lyrics came about from Matthew 18. Of course, I agreed.

This was new pathway formed by the pull of others through music. And I think another lesson from Matthew 18 is evidenced in this next step for Mom's hymn. For who would have thought the ten years of silence from this little hymn since Mom's death would now be graced with new life, new relationships and meanings for others?

~ ~ ~

Why This Word "Others" is Important

Two reasons stand out. One, of all the situations, books and other media, and possible learning tools we are exposed to, none are as powerful as other people. Grandmothers usually rate high on the influential scale, perhaps because they are usually mature and they usually have time to spend with us as we grow.

Secondly, others provide us with the opportunity help them, and experience the joys of giving of ourselves to assist someone else. There is a popular suggestion which is very true. If you feel gloomy, find someone else who is also gloomy and cheer them up. You will lose your gloom. If you feel agitated and anxious, find someone else who is experiencing similar feeling and help them become calm and refocused. You will experience the same calm and focus. If you're feeling pity for yourself, offer a prayer of thanksgiving for as many items and people in your life as you can think of. Pity will leave the room, because it cannot stand to be near thanksgiving.

What I said back in the Word Three DREAM chapter may now make more sense; "discover your personal passions. Then build your life around what you can do best for others through those passions. That will be your very special winning combination."

~ ~ ~

10 - THE TENTH WORD

"SYSTEMIC"

The symphony of systems and sub-systems work seamlessly as a whole to express and carry forth the intent and mission of its being.

The Extra Player in Systemic Groups

Ever heard the fifth voice in a quartet? Wait a minute, you say. A quartet has only four voices. Of course you are correct. But when listening to near-flawless harmonizing in quartets, you will also often hear the sum of the four, which will actually sound like a fifth voice. Ever notice that?

We can sense the same among certain sports teams. Team members of winning teams often radiate a high level team spirit, confidence, skills and comradeship. You can see it in individual players, but if you step back and look at the team as a whole, you may also sense the team spirit as an additional force, which it so often is.

Several years ago, I wrote a brief letter/article about my experience at a highly systemic restaurant. It was published in the Richmond Times-Dispatch as the Correspondent of the Day on 9/15/2007. Here it is: "Recently I had dinner at a favorite restaurant. From my seat, I could see the waiters, service expediters, bus staff, and other customers. It was as though I was watching a symphony unfold. All of the employees were urgently attending assignments, briskly greeting customers in passing, and whisking steaming plates to their destinations. They knew exactly what they were doing.

As I sat there, I realized that the staff, just like the recipes, the personnel policies, and the accounting systems are all so very important. Yet none of these, in reality, is the company behind this. These elements are simply trails left by the company. Even the most revealing of trails, the creative ideas and dreams of this symphony, are still not the company. For the company is more advanced and technically evasive. The company is that ever-changing assembly of proactive relationships, glued together by a mysterious love, which collectively drives these trails. When we try to cast the company as a group of people, or any other trail -- the real company slips under the door and moves on.

It occurred to me that the same is true of our enamored focus on the theory of evolution as an end in itself. Evolution, as the wholly systemic origin of species, is instead a trail of a company, a sub-operating procedure from a larger cosmic company. The theory of evolution remains an imperfect and fractional accounting system, a broken trail that mankind has yet to fully reconcile without applying a type of technological faith. Trails, like shadows, may be intellectually stimulating for what they appear to imitate. But, like the steam rising from a just-delivered steak, none of these is the company.

My meal was absolutely superb -- another grand-slam product of this company. But it is not the company."

~ ~ ~

Systemic Networks

They hovered over the warm vapors rising from the sunlit grass slope just outside of my studio. Clusters of swarming gnats in an apparent feeding frenzy were enjoying a picnic of nutrient-rich rising moisture. I had seen those dozens of times before, but today I saw something I had missed during all those other times.

Today, I stared in amazement at the individual clusters of gnats, each cluster about two feet wide and about three to four feet tall, and each containing hundreds of gnats swirling about. I wondered what kept them together in the clusters. I could see four clusters today, as they floated nearby, maintaining the general size of each cluster. At one point I saw one cluster actually drift through another one, coming out on the other side still intact. And the stationary cluster was still there too – as if nothing had happened. This was incredible, and I wondered – how can they sustain such intense group formations?

I noted light gray specks in the cluster. Each speck is a blur of the movement of a small gnat in this vertical cluster. Are these social insects? Or, are they simply responding to the boundaries of warm vapors? If they were grouped according to vapor clouds, one would think that the clusters would swell and shrink according to the moisture clouds formations and variations caused by the wind. But they don't. The clusters remain about the same size. Perhaps their size is based on the flying distance from one side of the cluster to the other and from the top to the bottom. To what great lengths does God go in the creation of his critters?

But then, I saw the most astonishing feat of all, and which I had never noticed before. That was the movement patterns within and of the individual clusters. I was so surprised at what I saw, that I observed them several other times on different days to confirm that such was happening. The gnats actually move in three distinct ways.

1 – They move individually, within the cluster, flying in what appears to be a random swirling fashion, but very rarely outside of the cluster.

2 – They move with the cluster, as if following a leader gnat, similar to the "V" shaped flocks of geese, pelicans, and other birds flying together. One can observe the birds for example – when the leader turns left, they all follow in a rhythm sequence,

each following from the front of the formation to the back. In a matter of seconds, the entire flock shape bends and heads off in a new direction. The gnats' clusters move in a similar way, bending in motion, each gnat taking a signal from nearby gnats and making the bending formation as it changes in directions. The leader(s) appear to be near the top, for most of the bending of the clusters I observed started at the top.

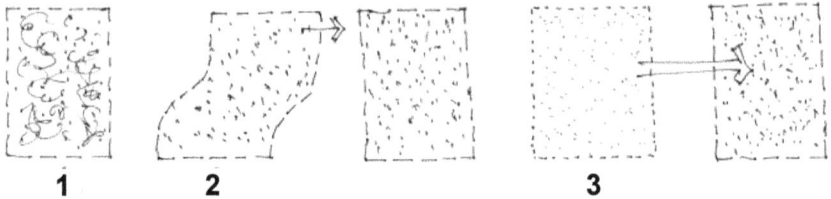

1   **2**   **3**

3 – And, amazingly, the clusters also move swiftly and uniformly as an entire unit – with no bending. That is, they all move within the cluster in what appears to be instant direction change communication. A cluster will instantly move to the right or left about two feet or so, as if the cluster is one unified gnat. This is remarkable and unbelievable.

Yet we see similar movement within schools of fish. You may have noticed – an entire school will move instantly and simultaneously to the left or to the right. At one point it was thought that the fish were actually following a leader, as in the type 2 movement above. But the latest thinking on fish school movement is that they have highly responsive senses, including sight, sound, smell and perhaps even a form of telepathy that they can switch on and off to a group mode. When it is switched on, all eyes see essentially as one, all sound is heard as if by one ear, and certain other perceptions of fear or food are sensed as one. Accordingly, when that "one" network of senses, made up of many individual senses, perceives a reason to move left, every fish moves left simultaneously. The gnats apparently have the same God-gifted ability, as that of about 80% of all fish -- the full understanding of which remains a mystery to us.

We may never fully understand how this miraculous communication works. We know humans rarely behave this way, unless it is a rehearsed routine such as performed by a marching band at half-time, for example, or a group dance. How significant it would be if we were able to react unrehearsed, similar to the gnats or fish, in an automatic group mode in our families, our businesses and educational organizations, and churches? What an immense improvement in unity and performance such may foster. Actually, like the gnats paralleling the schooled fish networking, we do have certain human examples in our own group actions that do come fairly close. Maybe we can learn something from them as well from the gnats. God may have purposely made it more challenging to us. For, we have to find and cultivate our group switch, and then learn how to turn it on.

If you have ever played doubles tennis, for example, you no doubt eventually found the "outside of yourself" switch, and you most likely learned how to turn it on. When that happened, you and your partner began acting more like "one" in response to the play than two separate individuals. Some players call the state "in the zone." They don't have or need the time during play to analyze each shot coming across the net. They just instinctively "know" what to do. The two respond to outside stimuli (the ball) in a fashion very similar to the way clustered gnats or schooled fish in the group mode respond to their outside stimuli (food, fear of predators, etc.) The same group mode switch appears to happen in good marriages too. Even in businesses and in small groups of friends. The group mode switch is discovered and turned on. But, what is the switch?

The switch is developed and nurtured – when we learn to quiet the mind and focus on communicating from and through the heart – from one heart to another. Yes, through the heart. Because the heart is also the seat of love, communications flow outward with a stamp of integrity and high receptivity that is rarely possible through brain-only communication. Heart communication is the purest and usually void of deception. Because of that it's also the fastest human way to truly communicate. It happens when your doubles tennis partner and you "know" rather than "think" the same play-thoughts. It happens when one spouse finishes the other's sentences, or when one business associate fills in for another, instantly without being asked. Asking is slow mental communication. It happens when a group of friends responds almost simultaneously to the needs of one who is down, hurt or not well. Perhaps equally important as physical skills in playing doubles tennis, using your heart and your partner's heart through nearly instant communications may be the fastest way to win. The same is true among football teams, marriage, families, career teams, church groups, life. Our group mode switch is in and through the heart.

How do we turn it on for communications? The same way we learned other procedures. Practice. Practice. Practice. Some people speak from their heart from the day they were born. Their group mode switch seems to always be on by default. I was lucky enough to marry one. The rest of us need to practice, for our group mode switch often appears to be off by default. Maybe God wanted us to discover it and learn how to activate it. While discussing this among a few friends, some told me they found a group mode (heart communication) switch by example, by observing others over time. Some told me they just figured it out through their own trials and errors, and eventually realized that the heart route is a vital part of a fulfilling life. Others told me they found they could activate their heart communications switch through their church, prayer, friends and their love for God – "with all of our heart...and all of our soul." Once they found it, continual practice moved them closer to the clustered gnats networking abilities. As proclaimed by the Apostle Paul through his seven books in the New Testament (some scholars believe he wrote as many as thirteen), all of the books nurture actions from the heart as one of the goals of the Christian lifestyle.

Just the other day, I watched again as a gnat cluster switched back and forth from moving as a unit for a few seconds, to the cluster bending motion, then back as a unit again. I could almost hear the switch clicking. Suppose, I wondered, the clusters were groups of senators, deacons, a Board of Trustees, or council members, or UN ambassadors? Suppose it's you and I, and a few others on a committee? Suppose it's two spouses in a difficult marriage?

Watching the gnat clusters demonstrate their highly-tuned networking abilities reminds me of the first two purposes in Rick Warren's book, The Purpose Driven Life. To love God and each other. In loving God we are reminded to "love God with all of our heart..." In loving each other, we are challenged to strive for unity in our own clustering. Perhaps one of the revelations of the gnats living out their networking capabilities right before us, is to provide us with such an example. Do you see other metaphors in gnat clusters? Their three states?

The heart, as our cluster switch, is also the part of us in which we are gifted invisible golden strings connecting us with God. Communicating with God through our heart and those special golden strings is a human natural – like the gnats in motion number 3. It's where we can "get in the zone" with God and absorb glimpses of His plan for us -- and "know" important pathways to take ahead, one step at a time. It is a pure and inherently more loving process than trying to live through the head and the brain only, where the ego is throned. The brain is certainly necessary. It is the engine of practical work. The heart, however, is God's guest room – where all things are possible.

~ ~ ~

Prayer: Systemic Subatomic Communication?

It was November 1995. Yet, I still can smell the medicinal tang floating in the Intensive Care Unit. I can still feel the dozens of tubes and wires clasping my body like insect legs, while beeps in the background dotted my semi consciousness. I wondered if I had been run over by a truck. Then, I remembered the open-heart triple bypass surgery I surrendered to earlier that morning. When I tried to ask a question, all I heard was some idiot blabbing with a mouth full of cotton.

I could see members of my family standing in a haze at the foot of my bed, smiling at me. I gave them the thumbs up sign and started to ask if they were okay, but the babbling idiot broke in again, chewing marbles. I wondered why they didn't get that guy out of here, and put me in a quieter cubical in this ICU.

The next morning it was a lot better. I reached for the phone, and a nurse rushed over to me and asked what in the world was I trying to do now. I didn't understand the "now" part, but I told her I wanted to call my wife to let her know I was okay. "It's 3:30 in the morning!" she said. "Oh," I sighed. I settled for what looked like a TV remote, and tried to change the channels of several TVs hanging over my bed. They all had picture problems, just waves and numbers -- and the remote didn't work.

Several hours later, after the change in nurse shifts, I reached for the phone again, and a new nurse helped me make the call. Kate, my wife, was shocked awake thinking it was a dire emergency. When she heard my voice saying, "Just wanted to let you know I'm doing fine," she thought maybe I had the wrong surgery. This was very invasive surgery, where the surgeons break the rib cage at the breast bone, then pry it apart using similar equipment used to open jammed doors in auto crashes, all to gain clear access to the heart and adjoining arteries. I was supposed to be in pretty bad shape this early after surgery, but I actually felt pretty good now. Later, I skipped the transition from

ICU to the next care level (to the joy of a few nurses) and instead went directly to a standard room. Several days later, I went home. I was very surprised at how well I continued to progress. The following Sunday I went to church and saw one of my grandsons dedicated. Our minister, mentioned during the service that he was surprised to see me this soon after surgery, and I said "Me too, but I couldn't miss seeing this dedication service." Silently I wondered, "How could this be?"

How could my recovery be so quick and positive? By the grace of God, something beyond the surgeons' skills and my own health and immune system had happened here. Something else was going on. Soon I got a revealing hint in the mail. When I opened the envelope at home, I saw a batch of prayer cards signed personally by members of our church. They had, unknowingly to me, prayed for me during two prayer meetings. Although I didn't have any scientific proof that such was the reason for my abnormal recovery, I knew instantly in my heart when I saw the prayer cards -- and the individual handwritten signatures, that such was the case. I will be forever grateful for their intercessory love and prayers. This was the beginning of a life-changing experience for me.

Later I learned that Dr. Larry Dossey, a Dallas physician and author of eight books, had documented case after case throughout the USA and abroad, in double blind studies, of actual medical benefits of prayer during surgery in situations very similar to mine. A large majority of patients who were unaware of others praying for them, consistently had faster and healthier recoveries than those who were not prayed for. Those prayed-for patients, when they later learned of the study, were just as surprised and moved by the experience as I. In his 1989 book, Recovering the Soul, Dr. Dossey explained the concept of "nonlocal mind" – intelligence unconfined to the brain and body, a mind spread infinitely throughout space and time. To Christians, this is a beginning description of God and the Trinity. And, since God remains accessible to all humans, the term "nonlocal mind" serves as a generic source for Dossey's medical work (mission) and the process of prayer. The scientific evidence of God's implicate mechanisms of prayer is a mission tool for Dossey, just as it is for Christians under-girded by our own faith, and is available to us in working with all people along their own individual paths.

~ ~ ~

The Systemic Nature of the Universe

On another scientific path, the late David Bohm, a groundbreaking quantum physicist, awakened much of the science world with his Theory of Implicate Order and other bridges between science and spirit. In 1982 a remarkable experiment by Bohm's colleagues, including colleagues of the late Albert Einstein, showed that subatomic particles that are far apart (nonlocal) are able to communicate in ways that cannot be explained by the transfer of physical signals traveling at or slower than the speed of light. This is where Dossey's and Bohm's work converge. Subsequent subatomic communications including subatomic "adjustments" are what Christians describe as answers to prayers. According to my interpretations of Dossey's and Bohm's work and proven conclusions, that is exactly what happened to me during and after surgery -- subatomic particle adjustments were set into motion through subatomic nonlocal particle communication between those praying for me and God.

Such subatomic communication, according to Bohm's and many other scientists' findings, is absolutely instant, while all other forms of particle or wave communication (travel) is believed by most scientist to be limited to the speed of light. Isn't it interesting how God, in His intricate and infinite creation, set a speed limit on all forms of travel and communication, except those to and from His implicate-order infinite-mind?

Bohm's ideas are further underlined by his remark, "...the implicate domain (higher order) could equally well be called Idealism, Spirit, Consciousness. The separation of the two – matter and spirit – is an abstraction..." Christians, Jews and other religions of the world, of course, have known this for thousands of years. Now it is confirmed through quantum physics.

Prayer then, may be "technically" defined as a process of aligning with the implicate domain and then sharing in the universally granted instant communication of nonlocal information by thought and focused intention. This process of prayer is scientifically proven to work (Dossey) and transpire in a detectable yet mysterious form of communication (Bohm).

Accordingly, we welcome "brother science" here. Sometimes you are slow -- very slow. But eventually you seem to arrive at part of the truth, evidenced now at the quantum level and based on the limited type of information you seek. Yes, keep plugging. As we will. Thanks for the prayer wink. Thanks even more to our implicate domain God for prayer -- from someone who carries a most grateful and now stronger beating interest in bouncing this double-edged loving truth to others.

So what does this mean to believers? Probably little in terms of one's own specific beliefs, although it offers us another opportunity to smile. As believers we draw upon own source of faith and evidence from our personal relationship with our God of the implicate order. We also draw upon the Bible, prayer, our experiences through worship services and other church activities. But, there are two powerful reasons this prayer-science subject is of interest to me and hopefully to some of you. One, this scientific news can have significant positive impact upon our work with non-believers. Two, the scientific evidence may eventually have a positive impact upon public policy-making, such as prayer in schools and the workplace.

A number of those who make or influence public policies for the rest of us, including our children and grandchildren, are non-believers, some claiming to be atheists (denying the existence of God) or, agnostics (those who believe that there can be no proof of the existence of God, but do not deny the possibility that God exists) or, "almost believers." These folks are generally well educated, smart, and proactive in areas that affect many, including politics, law and legislation. Many of them are friends and co-workers. Some may be loved ones or family. All of them are God's children.

Many of these non-believer leaders may not be aware of the relatively recent science discoveries -- suggesting that we are all surrounded by an invisible, yet sparkling spiritual soup – a highly systemic spiritual soup radiant with subatomic particles which have direct cell-phone-like connections with God (the implicate domain). The Bible describes this spiritual soup often as angel armies of God.

Believers are urged by the apostle Paul to "pray without ceasing" – to keep our spiritual cell phones on and close to our soul's ears, so that we may continually dialogue with God. God has graced us with a trinity of cell phone connections; God the Father, God the Son Jesus, and God the Holy Spirit, the friend that Jesus said He would send after His ascension. We are further blessed, for as we connect with one of these, we connect with all three.

Thus we might consider in our work with non-believers and "almost" believers, that science's evidence on prayer may serve as a new "John the Baptist" forerunner of the next step story for them. Such evidence may help pave the way for open minds and hearts to deeper truths. Having science as one of our missionaries can be a very valuable tool in our service to others.

With that in mind, let's consider a third scientist's view of spiritual systemic evidence, prayer, through the work of Andrew Newberg, M.D., professor of nuclear medicine at the University of Pennsylvania Medical Center. He has become a rising star in the field of neurotheology, the brain science behind spiritual and religious experience. In an article, "This is Your Brain Praying" in the January-February, 2004 issue of Spirituality & Health, Louise Danielle Palmer describes her interview with Newberg regarding his work. Among her comments, she mentions his scanning the brains of a group of Franciscan nuns during moments of profound contemplative prayer. The scans were almost identical to a previous scan of a group of Buddhists monks in prayer, both indicating the thalamus in participants was actually asymmetrical, suggesting that the brain structure of serious spiritual practitioners differs from most people's. This suggests that prayer not only produces documented benefits (Dossey), but also its continued practice may actually refine our brain structure. Newberg also learned that the consistent and universal human longing to connect with something larger than ourselves is grounded in our biology and manifested in the wiring of the brain. This suggests that not only does the process scientifically thrive, but also we need it. It also suggests that prayer in itself is not a religion.

Science, as we will ultimately see in time, is all Christians' friend. For it is like God's librarian. It reports on and catalogs our growing yet limited knowledge of God's amazing and intricate mechanisms – whether orbiting planets in space, the structure of a bloom, or now the human prayer process. Likewise, science is becoming the atheists' enemy, and it will continue to unfold hard supportive evidence sufficient for the most spiritual-deaf non-believer, in scientific gut-wrenching revelations -- which will eventually dissolve the already non-scientific "belief" in self-only intelligence. In the meantime, prayer has already crossed over into the scientific log book. Prayer is real (Bohm). It works (Dossey). Everyone needs it (Newberg).

Based on these few examples, and much other evidence not mentioned here, the concluding implications are strong. While this may not be spiritual news to believers, the hard evidence regarding prayer offers us new opportunities to work with non-believers; and, new opportunities for us to correct prayer policies in public places. This are the two primary points I wish to make in this two-part reference to the systemic of prayer.

Anti-prayer groups' key witness (science) has now moved to our believers' table. We must move to restore prayer as a proven scientific and universal process back into our schools and the workplaces. There are, of course two separate issues here. One is banning the practice of forced belief systems and their practices onto others, particularly in public supported and/or participated events. That stands as said, including the non-scientific atheists' "belief" systems.

Prayer itself, however, is not a religion. It is a human process, like blinking, or smiling. It is only when blinking, for example, is exercised in a particular religious ritual, and forced on others to observe or participate as part of a specific religion, should it be subject to restrictions. Communication between non-local particles, however, as a process of meditation, intuition, is simply an intrinsic process, by whatever name one wishes to call it. It is a scientific benefit-procedure, like breathing, and thus the process itself should NOT be restricted. Ever.

To disregard the technical actuality of this process and its proven benefits is scientific and human ignorance, just as banning deep breathing before an exam, or banning warm-ups before a track event. In fact, public educational systems, as any educational system, have a responsibility to lay this out for students and provide labs for experiments of the process.

The process itself is not a "religion." We use the prayer process in our religion, in our intercessory concern for others, as Jesus taught, and we use it in our daily walks with our Lord, as Paul instructed the early Christians. But we also use hugs, smiles and love for others. Prayer, like love and joy, is an important expression and communicative processes in our religion. But these procedures themselves are not our religion. Attempting to ban hugs (for example) or any of these human intrinsic processes, would be in itself a form of a "religion." And, recent scientific evidence contradicts entirely the authority to do so.

I can imagine 15 years from now, just before commencement, the announcer saying, "Let's pause for SNPC" (Subatomic Nonlocal Particle Communication). Students, in this admittedly imaginative scene, would know exactly what that means, because SNPC is a required course, just like health and math. Students might explain it to parents, just as they do now about computers and racial prejudice. They might explain it the same way they reply to someone complaining that chemistry class is offensive. Or, football practice. Or, consuming oxygen. Get real.

While we add these science revelations to our mission toolkit, might we also strive to help our public policies "get real" by passing on the need for legislators and others to update their understanding of recent scientific evidence on prayer? We can help by unfolding recent scientific and theological information to our children and grandchildren, so that they may be equipped to understand the process and benefits of prayer. We can help by supporting groups and elected officials who are proactively working to remove the ban on prayer in our public places. We can help by dialoging on the issues and sharing our thoughts with others.

Unfeasible?

Impossible? Unscientific?
Questionable in fact?
While we yawn at the opening of a rose,
and bore at spontaneous remission,
deadly diseases vaporize instantly
and unscientifically.
We miss the Butterfly.

Surely, science is a narrow tool choice
for exploring unknown possibilities,
just as it was when, left behind, rotting
on those Spanish docks, it was caught
in the warm back-draft of the same wind
which captured the sails and hearts
of those abandoning flat-earth logic,
following a deeper knowing.

How then do we find it easier to acknowledge
without skepticism -- even that fish
breathe in water, yet suffocate in air?

How can we accept -- unquestioningly
the delicate yet constant unwavering balance
of atmospheric nitrogen and oxygen
surrounding planet Earth here,
despite our brutality and technical nods,
though a minor tweak in percentages
would be catastrophic?

Tis it easier to brush aside too
without wonder, an infant's smile,
or the minuscule details
of a newborn's hand, and fingers
and tiny intricate fingernails?

Or ignore the melody of spring,
the majestic quiet of snow,
while we sway with stupor under the moon
as it pulls the tides with unseen grace,
beyond black holes and quasars,
among quantum non-local particles
which somehow converse in physics' soup?

When I consider such, while the animals
still detect earthquakes, hours before
highly sensitive equipment awakens--
even as salmon, pigeons, whales and others
play with navigational systems
which dwarf our most advanced
instruments of tinkering...

I reason in this limited way,
nudged by the winds of the soul–
that resurrection of God's chosen
is technologically God's piece of cake,
a medical breeze in this cosmos of
energy-packed, passion-giving systems,

bent on unfolding unconditional love

in its ongoing story – over and over,

even among our lethargic frowns

and embryonic science.

~ ~ ~

Anyone Can Lead Until...

One of the core problems in our culture today can be summarized in two phrases behind a common acronym. The first phrase is, "Anyone Can Lead Until..." For example, Hitler led... until the world put a stop to it. Japan led... until the world put a stop to it. Al Capone and his mob led.... until the USA put a stop to it. The point is, the existence of a leading influence is not an indication that it will continue, or that it is correct or God-based. If its roots do not sink into God's soil, sooner or later, someone will put a stop to it.

The second phrase associated with this same embedded acronym, is "American Civil Liberties Union." Yes, ironically ACLU is an acronym for both of these phrases. The ACLU serves a valuable purpose of protecting human civil liberties. Sometimes, however, the ACLU steps beyond its original and very sound fundamentals and squints in near blind un-civil fuzziness into scenes beyond its theater. In those situations it too now exemplifies "Anyone Can Lead Until...we put a stop to it."

The case in point is the ACLU attempting to take Christ out of Christmas, and God out of the workplace, school place and even aiming at taking God out of the home place. Their operating power comes from dangling fears of threatened lawsuits over businesses, school boards, universities and all of those who don't follow "their" rules -- a process which strikes chords similar to the old mobster insurance plans.

Although recent polls[1] confirm that over 80% of the USA population believe in God, that 80% continues to allow a small group of lawyers with largely unsupported agendas to push the rest of the USA to the limit to "support" (not just provide civil liberties) for a small fraction of the population who claim to be atheist. Since it is impossible to prove that God does NOT exist, "Atheistism" is actually a belief system. Thus, it is a rare type of self-religion. As such, providing covenants and special provisions for their (exclusive) civil liberties while offending 80% of the population and their beliefs by specifically excluding them, is unquestionably unconstitutional. The only constitutional answer is to "allow" all religions free expression, which is what the Fathers of the Constitution intended. Religions ARE separate from government – UNTIL government focuses its low spectrum eyes on any one of them. Then, government steps over the Constitution and attempts to peek into the forbidden trying to understand what it cannot possibly grasp -- like a steel beam trying to understand music.

It is time for the 80% of the USA to rise to the occasion and stop these un-civil efforts. For enough is enough and we need to put a stop to it. A good example of such efforts is found through the late Dr. James Kennedy's work with five other founding leaders. I urge all to check out what those six and their group of Christian lawyers began in 1994 as the Alliance Defense Fund (ADF)[2] which continues today to strongly defend and defeat increasing numbers of ACLU lawsuits. I urge you to check this out and support their efforts.

[1]*Darren Sherkat, Southern Illinois University; General Social Surveys, National Opinion Research Center, as referenced in The Christian Century magazine, December 14, 2004 issue.*

[2]*Alliance Defense Fund on the web at*
http://en.wikipedia.org/wiki/Alliance_Defense_Fund and
http://www.AllianceDefenseFund.org/

Why This Word "SYSTEMIC" is Important

This is a "big picture" word and often we don't recognize the huge quantity of systems that surround achievement and success. McDonald's is a good example of a highly systemic operation on multiple levels. They systemize everything from the menu, to the delivery, storage and preparation of its products to how they treat customers. When they opened franchises, now world-wide, it provided not only ways to expand, but further golden opportunities to test and tweak all of their systems. They are systemic because such is a much more efficient, economical and customer-pleasing way to operate. They are more successful financially by being highly systemic. And the food taste better.

We personally should especially systemize all of those things we don't enjoy doing. Figure out and practice the best possible way you can accomplish it. Then do it that way. You will spend far less time doing it, and also far less time re-doing it.

Many small and medium-sized businesses, churches, schools, associations and even institutions can benefit greatly by further systemizing their operations. I have observed organizations, businesses and churches that appear to have started last week. They still haven't figured out the best way to do hardly anything. Everything appears to be a "first time I've done that" routine. So, it takes much longer to do things, it cost much more, and it probably keeps either customers and/or other employees waiting in the process. But the most serious result of operations and people settling for non-systemic procedures is that they greatly lower their mission achievement and accomplishment levels. On the other hand, highly successful businesses and organizations, just like highly successful sports teams, run like a clock.

~ ~ ~

"COINCIDENCE"

Usually most coincidences aren't.

Kennedy and Lincoln

The following story has many variations. People keep finding or sometimes making up similarities between Kennedy and Lincoln. Even considering a possible 5% - 10% error, this is still amazing. Are they accidental events or something else?

Abraham Lincoln was elected to Congress in 1846.

John F Kennedy was elected to Congress in 1946.

Abraham Lincoln was elected President in 1860.

John F. Kennedy was elected President in 1960.

Both were particularly concerned with civil rights.

Both wives lost their children while living in the White House.

Both Presidents were shot on a Friday.

Both Presidents were shot in the head.

Lincoln's secretary was named Kennedy.

Kennedy's Secretary was named Lincoln.

Both were assassinated by Southerners.

Both were succeeded by Southerners named Johnson.

Andrew Johnson, who succeeded Lincoln, was born in 1808.

Lyndon Johnson, who succeeded Kennedy, was born in 1908.

John Wilkes Booth, who assassinated Lincoln, was born in 1839.

Lee Harvey Oswald, who assassinated Kennedy,

was born in 1939.

Both assassins were known by their three names.

Both names are composed of fifteen letters.

Lincoln was shot at the theater named 'Ford.'

Kennedy was shot in a car called 'Lincoln' made by Ford

Booth ran from the theater and was caught in a warehouse.

Oswald ran from a warehouse and was caught in a theater.

Booth and Oswald were assassinated before their trials.

Author(s) unknown

~ ~ ~

Tax Day

It began as a normal Monday morning, I thought. Other than being "Tax Day", the news didn't describe today, April 15th, with any great significance. Yet, I had a strange and uneasy feeling.

I started my NordicTrack exercise routine. Usually I begin earlier, but this morning, it was almost 7:30. I hooked up my tape and earphones -- to listen to an audio book and focus my mind upon more interesting subjects, far beyond the exercise routine.

Today, I thought I would probably finish the four-tape audio book on Lincoln, by David Herbert Donald. I had ordered the tape about three months before, and had been listening to it from time to time, as the mood struck. I remembered I had quit near the end of the last tape. The Civil War had just concluded, and Lincoln was uncharacteristically jubilant. He finally had good reason. The last of the violence and bloodshed was at hand, he thought. And, today, somehow, it seemed strange that I would hear again the destiny of that sad episode in our history.

I checked the clock again and noted the time in my memory. I use the clock to double-check my duration with the mileage logged by the machine. I wouldn't want to punish myself too long, of course. Now, I started the tape and the NordicTrack; it was 7:30 a.m. exactly.

Soon, my body began to heat up and I heard the plots of John Wilkes Booth. How he initially planned to kidnap the president, then changed his mind after hearing the president's last speech. Booth declared that it would, in fact, be his very last. A few minutes later on the tape, I heard Mr. Lincoln beginning what was to be a long and tragic day. I listened as he went through the meetings, his private carriage trip around town with his wife, Mary. Then, more daily meetings, more papers to sign – and, finally, his evening trip to the theater.

I kept plodding away on the NordicTrack -- following every detail of the familiar story. Lincoln was seated in his Presidential Box. Then, John Wilkes Booth slipped in and waited for just the right moment. As the crowd roared with laughter at one part in the performance, Booth aimed and fired one shot from his Derringer pistol into Lincoln's head only 24 inches away. The president jolted forward and fell mortally wounded, slumped over the balcony railing. Moments later, to the horror of the theater goers, his barely-alive body was carried across the street to a guest room in a neighbor's home. Doctors gathered desperately struggling to turn the tide against the unrelenting fate. After appraising the severe head injury, they estimated he would live no more than a couple of hours.

The tape story continued. Mr. Lincoln persisted and lingered on and on. I knew the general story-line but I didn't remember all the specifics. When I heard the date and time, I suddenly stopped the NordicTrack. In a flash, I felt as though I were there, 150 years ago. My consciousness zoomed to Washington, brushing by those gathered around Mr. Lincoln. Vapors of gloom swirled around us. The only sounds came from the book tape navigating us through the process. My physical body stood motionless on the NordicTrack, still holding the cross-country ski ropes out in front of me. Sweaty heat rose past my face, drawing with it waves of sadness and wrenching despair. But, in that guest room, I felt a strange urge to say, "Receive our honor and love for you, Mr. Lincoln." So I did. And again. Suddenly, the scene was all gone, and I was back home on the NordicTrack.

I stood there dumbfounded -- by the details I had just witnessed -- the glimmering color in the blood-soaked bed linens, and tides of bottomless grief and waves of sorrow I felt with everyone in that crowded room. I staggered again at the exact time and date of his death as I heard the tape summarize the facts of this synchronized finale, now with music in the background. "Mr. Lincoln was shot. He died nine hours later, the next morning, on April 15th at 7:30 a.m."

~ ~ ~

Human performance DNA – The EMA Cycle

About 10 years into running my architectural practice of about 18 employees, I discovered the EMA Cycle. Many of our staff were recent graduate architects aspiring to be creative. That's why I hired them. One of my primary roles was to support and nurture them so they could provide the highest level of services for our clients.

That year, we tried a new procedure. Early in the schematic design phase, I asked the architect assigned to the project to give the rest of us architects a brief presentation in the conference room of the owner's program, the budget, the timeframe and initial ideas with sketches showing how we could accomplish those goals for our client. At first, these presentations were discovery exercises for us, but then the real discoveries soon began to happen.

As the young architects unfolded their ideas for their projects, colleagues grew very comfortable and appreciative in being included in the important formative stages of the projects. I remember comments like, "I like the way you arranged the entrance to the building." Or, "The way you have scoped out the program and budget – with this general design, looks like the project will have the funds to use high quality materials. The client will be very proud of that. I will too. Good ideas."

I wish you could have seen the bright eyes of the young project architects at these sessions. Comments like that were exactly what they needed to hear. And they were right. Colleagues also had suggestions, and all were made in a positive light. At times, I actually felt a little choked up over what I was witnessing, just as I am now in recalling those sessions of many years ago. We were making an important discovery there. Months later I wrote about these sessions and presented what we were learning at one of the University of Wisconsin seminars for architects and engineers. The attendees were very interested to learn that we were practicing what I called the EMA Cycle – Express, Measure, Adjust.

This EMA Cycle is a key process which helps facilitate higher personal creativity, increased performance, executive relational skills, career opportunities as well as (beyond the office) improved parenting skills, personal relationships, and many other aspects of the human experience. The Cycle is a three-step process, the first and third steps of which are automatically energized by humans – provided the middle step, the non-automatic one, is purposely supplied and activated by other people and systems. But, whenever that middle step (M) is missing -- when it is NOT fully supplied and supported by employers, managers, sponsors, coaches, teachers, parents, and other human resource staff, the performing recipient's automatic first (E) and third (A) steps may soon fade, eventually deteriorate and disappear.

How do the three steps work in this process, this EMA Cycle?

E (in the EMA) = Express. You hit the golf ball. You write a sentence. You draw a sketch. You greet a friend. Imagine how many "E's" you practice and process every day. We express naturally. Generally, people are employed or commissioned and paid for their "E's".

M = Measure. You naturally seek to measure the trajectory and angle of that golf ball you just hit, compared with where you wanted it to go. You re-read that sentence you just wrote, against what you intended to say. You observe (and quickly wonder about) the friend's facial expression following your greeting. In this step, we can only estimate or guess at the measurements of our own expression, but answers coming from other people, special measurement systems, cameras, etc. are much more believable to us and more likely to automatically trigger the next step, which is:

A = Adjust. Based on one's perceived (and preferred supplemental) measurement results of the previous expression (ie, the golf ball's travel) how would you now adjust your next expression to generate a better result? Would you grip the golf club any differently? If so, how? Would you swing differently? How? What did your measurement step tell you? Not much? Or, volumes of information? Do you begin to see the potential here for systemic feedback?

We actually see these EMA Cycles in continuous operation in all sports. Consider football, for example. Imagine a running back has just been given the ball on the defender's 40 yard line. His blockers are ahead of him; they swing to right. It's third down and about 6 yards to go. He is concentrating on making a first down. He glances over at the first down sidelines flag marker. He sets in his mind on the yard line he must cross in order to make that first down. But what would happen, if, suddenly all of the yard markers disappeared, and all of the sideline markers and first down flags disappeared as well? The running back would suddenly finds himself running "blindly" in a field of "no measurements."

The important questions for us at this point are, in the real game of football, how many first downs would be missed if at such moments, the players were denied that measurement step? How many "extra efforts" would be neutralized if the players were denied the benefit of seeing exactly where they must advance? In my experience many such achievements would be missed. The same is true in the office and at home.

Extra effort tends to be proportional with the level of the "M" – measurement phase, assuming other levels of physical ability, etc. are equal. Yet, we often mistakenly think that extra effort is essentially an "E" phase only. But in reality, we all need and crave the "M" phase, the yard markers, so we can "A" adjust accordingly and "E" again and again as we shoot for our own first down markers. Continuous EMA cycles are a sign of creativity, in running backs, architectural offices and at home.

If, however, the "M" phase stops or is not experienced, the cycle stops, or short-circuits, and creativity ceases. When we found in our office that certain design time budgets were exceeded, for example, it was NOT because someone was incapable or intended failure. Instead, it was simply because someone did not know where they were (time-wise) and where they needed to go to reach a goal. (Poor yard markers) Once I redesigned our time management systems around the EMA Cycle, things changed dramatically.

In my experience, businesses, friends and families which focus on providing good "M" points for each other, optimize helping people to spring into unlimited thrilled expressions. But if a person, family or organization instead supplies a substitute "E" or "A" point, it denies the internalizing of the expressing person's own "M" point, then usually the EMA cycle stops. We need to supply as many "M" points as possible to help each other meet that deep need so as to intrinsically move onto our next "A" and then begin another full EMA cycle. Can you see some of these ideas in the YOU chapter, the SPIRIT chapter and the DREAM chapter in this EMA Cycle?

So you might wonder why this EMA Cycle is in the COINCIDENCE chapter. First, perhaps you have noticed that all of the Twelve Words are interrelated. They are Systemic. As I was pondering where include the EMA Cycle, I remembered the Bible verse about loving our neighbor as we do ourselves. And, it is so true that a good way to honor and love someone is to provide "M"-- measurement points for them. Not "E" points for them and Not "A" points for them, but supply "M"-- measurement points for them. Practice this and see what happens. Instead of saying, "Nice to see you again," (boring), say something like, "That's the neatest tie I've seen in a long time." Watch his face. The next time one of your children or grandchildren completes even the slightest accomplishment, tell him or her (truthfully) that you liked the way he/she did something in a particular way. Watch the eyes. They are reflections of a soaring human spirit. It's a great and rewarding way to love our neighbors and our family as we do ourselves. Support them with what they need -- "M" points.

Coincidence? Certainly an initial value of a seemingly coincidental situation is that it gets our attention. I have found that upon further reflection, most coincidences aren't coincidental, but instead are expressions of a bigger story, which sometimes is beyond our capacity to understand. In this case I don't believe it is a coincidence that we are hard-wired with the EMA Cycle within, waiting to automatically thunder into action with a little love pat or tweak idea, and continue cycling highly productive routines as we find needed "M" points along the way. I think it is the way Universe is designed, a way to include and remind all of humanity that other people's inclusion helps to optimize our output. Love others by providing "M" points. That's one of the ways God loves us.

"Teacher, which command in God's Law is the most important?"

Jesus said, "'Love the Lord your God with all your passion and prayer and intelligence.' This is the most important, the first on any list. But there is a second to set alongside it: 'Love others as well as you love yourself.' These two commands are pegs; everything in God's Law and the Prophets hangs from them."
Matthew 22:36-40 (The Message)

~ ~ ~

Why "COINCIDENCE" is important

By definition, a coincidence is an accidental sequence of events that appear to have been caused by something else. So if one agrees that a certain series of events is a coincidence, then the person agrees that it was accidental. I have found that most coincidences aren't really coincidences. That is based on my own experience and subsequent events that then followed the apparent coincidence. You, no doubt, will be (or have been) confronted with numerous questionable coincidences as well. I view all of these as important, and I hope you will give them sufficient attention along with events or any nudges (possible "M" points) following to help you sense if some message(s) may be trying to get your attention. I often find that once a "coincidence" gets my attention, important messages, ideas or insights follow.

~ ~ ~

12 - THE TWELFTH WORD

"ACCOUNTABILITY"

Responsibility is accountability with a future.

Unaccountable, or Just a Dream?

I was partially awakened in the early morning by a dream, leaving me with the sense that I should pass this along, particularly to parents. In my dream I was witnessing another example of students being unprepared for life through wimpy educational practices, taking the classroom away from the teacher and awarding it to lofty teams of social-civil administrators. Soon a slogan emerged in my half-awakened mind. Just Flunk Them. Please. "JFT. Please."So, at least out of inconvenience, the students might try again, this time from within.

Then, I saw myself being waited on in a mall store by a high school student. My item purchase price was $12.76. I handed the student cashier $20.01, expecting change in the amount of $7.25. Instead, I saw a direct example of how many young parents shield their sons and daughters from learning the genuine way, in favor of the new protective way. As the student fumbled with sounds of agony and second grade arithmetic, there was a flash of that horror which all modern families are taught to fear like a broken cell phone – the loss of self confidence. But now it poured all over the counter, spilling onto the floor, seeping under the shoes of the poor dumb-founded youngster, who had been escorted onto life's race track without a thinking helmet, or even a steering wheel.

Now, I was waiting for the "victim response" so nurtured in the minds of our youth by guilt-ridden seldom home parents. But there was no verbal reply. Finally, in desperation, he looked up.

Blank. Our eyes met. Was that me in there? Is anyone in there? Hoping to avoid further pain to both of us, I said, "Seven dollars and a quarter."

"Sure," he mumbled, in a sweeping motion, as he gathered and passed me the change. Like, this is now history. Under the rug. Next, please.

As I stepped back and folded the seven dollars into my wallet, I noticed a handmade sign scribbled with a ball-point pen on the back of an envelope, leaning against the register. "Correct Change Appreciated."

Then I woke up. Mumbling, JFT, please. But, it was just a dream. Or, was it?

~ ~ ~

Accountability Guidelines for Personal Financial Management

Just after I married my bride, Kate, in 1960, my Dad pulled me aside one day at his home. He said he wanted to share with me a secret he developed when he and Mom got married almost 30 years before. My eyes widened with curious interest. He pulled out an old shoe box held together with rubber bands. As he slowly opened it, I saw a bunch of worn envelopes inside with a title written on each one.

"This is my budget system," Dad said. He showed me an envelope marked "Car," then another one marked "Groceries," and another one marked "Fun." There were several others. Most of them had cash inside.

"How does this work?" I asked.

"When I get paid each month," he explained, "I put some of the pay into our savings accounts and some into our checking account for fixed expenses like insurance. Then I take the remaining pay in cash and divide it up among these envelopes to help us manage our expenses. You see," he went on, "I put a certain budgeted amount in each of the envelopes here. We use the cash during the month. But when the grocery money is gone, that's all we can spend on groceries this month, unless we can spare or borrow some money from the other envelopes."

I thought that is pretty neat. Maybe I'll consider something like that someday. As it turned out, as every year went by, Dad's envelope system made more sense. It still does. Not only did it help him budget and pay day-to-day expenses, but it also provided instant feedback on how they were doing financially (accountability). When the grocery money was gone, it was gone. When the entertainment envelope was empty, it was empty until next month. These were very powerful yet simple management tools. That instant feedback that was available to him anytime during the month on how much of the budgeted amounts were left in each of the envelopes was a very important feature that today is missing in many families' spending.

Kate and I use a similar system today on the computer and a popular financial management software to manage all of our envelopes (as budget accounts) except cash spending. Our cash spending envelope is managed from my billfold and her purse, just like Dad's envelopes. Instant feedback. We use a budgeted weekly spending amount for entertainment, meals out, etc. That budgeted amount for cash is replenished each week. We refer to it, count it, and spend it cautiously as we enjoy every penny of it, never worrying about it.

Well, you might say, "Why not just use a debit card?" The answer is simple. Debit cards are financial traps, unless you carry with you at all times an up-to-date debit card ledger so you can post every purchase. The debit card alone provides no feedback whatsoever as to how much you have spent this week or this month. If you wait for the bank's monthly statement, it's too late to do any good. And, if you don't know how much you've spent, you will spend more. The banks know that, and that's why they love debit cards.

Well, you might say, "I can go online and find my bank balance in a matter of seconds." Sure you can, but that's a fictitious balance. It's not correct, because it may not have yet deducted your last several debit charges or outstanding checks you wrote which have not yet cleared the bank. So, if your online balance shows $200 and your not-yet cleared debits add up to $215.00, you are actually overdrawn by $15.00. And, banks love that too. The debit card is a very poor management tool, except for the bank. It improves their income. Who do you think pays for that added income? It's a poor financial tool for users because it does not provide users with feedback needed for accurate accountability. Debit cards, just like credit cards, encourage financial unaccountability.

Over the years Kate and I encouraged our kids to plan, budget and save for tomorrow as well as next week, monthly, annually, and for the future. As they each got married, we passed along these shoe box secrets from Dad including accounting for emergency funds, their children's college expenses, their own retirement and long term care costs.

The present economy confirms that we never really know what is going to happen. To help counter that with the best tools we can find, financial planners and family guidance literature strongly advises people to establish financial goals, career goals, budgets and savings plans as early as possible and continually update them. Let me add to that good advice by saying that whatever procedures and systems you set up, make sure they produce sufficient instant feedback in hands-on ways (like seeing the envelopes half empty) to give you the accountability you need in real time.

For many years, I have planned our retirement accounts and in the last ten years or so, as retirement has drawn closer, I have read and studied extensively on the subject. So now, here are some of the "I wish I had-of" thoughts and guidelines I have learned and would have begun as soon as I got out of college -- if I had it to do all over again. Consider these six guiding principles as you develop your own accountable family financial strategy. As always, I suggest you discuss these and your own ideas with your financial advisors.

Using the following guidelines is sort of like leaning how to ride a bike. If you follow certain basic principles (like turning the front wheel of the bike towards the direction you are beginning to fall) the bike will correct itself – and you can continue your journey without interruption. If however you instead turn the front wheel in the opposite direction of where you are beginning to fall, you and the bike will surely fall causing an interruption of your journey, and perhaps even injuries. Once you follow and adjust the guiding principles as required to maintain steady and safe speeds, and steer your bike in the direction you want to go (avoiding pot holes and ditches along the way) the riding soon becomes automatic. You just get on the bike and go – without thinking about it. Principle-based and exciting guided, accountable "financial riding" can happen the same way. It can become a part of your soul. It can become automatic, like bike riding, and you will never forget how it is done. But you have to learn how to ride first, and practice and practice.

Guiding principle 1: Set a family-nurturing income goal. Based on what I read and understand of minimum expenses at the time of this writing, it appears that a typical five-person family – father, mother and three children will need a combined **minimum** annual income in the range of $75,000 - 80,000, including taxes. Some of you may earn more than that, and maybe some of you believe that you can live on substantially less than that. However, my point here is that if you lower the required combined income by skipping one or more of the guiding principles here (such as not saving for emergencies) it will cost you more later. One of the things you should avoid is paying more through late fees, unnecessary interest and higher charges because you didn't plan adequately.

As many of you know (and I trust our grandchildren are learning this from their parents) paying interest on credit cards, or interest on loans for money that was not set aside earlier, always costs more in the long run. If you can't afford to pay off the credit card balance each month, then how can you afford to pay more later? That doesn't make sense. If you can't afford that either, then your credit card use is unaccountable, like a debit card. Spot that problem as early as you can and correct it promptly. Plan and seek income sources as required to provide the minimum combined income you and your family truly need to live accountably. Look at last year's total expenses, including loans, deferred expenditures you needed to make but maybe didn't because funds were not available. Add all of that up. <u>Arrive at a goal for your combined family-nurturing income</u>. Note, a realistic goal of your family-nurturing income is different from a "just getting by" income. You may need to make some income and career changes. See *It's Your Choice* in chapter 3, page 42.

Guiding principle 2: Set aside an emergency fund. As an essential part of your monthly budget, set aside (without fail) a small, fixed amount (or percentage of earnings) into a separate EMERGENCY money market account (at your bank). Build up this fund until you can maintain a minimum $5,000 balance in that account and NEVER use that money for anything except emergencies (major car repairs, replacing the water heater, etc.). Then, once any of that $5,000 is used, replenish the balance as quickly as possible. Otherwise you will begin to turn the front wheel of your financial bike in the wrong direction in this emergency situation.

Guiding principle 3: Set aside a big ticket fund. Another essential allocation of monthly income is setting aside (absolutely every month) a second small fixed amount (or percentage of earnings) into a second BIG TICKET money market account or Certificate of Deposit (CD) at your bank so that you can eventually maintain a second $5,000 (or more) minimum balance in that account and NEVER use that money for anything except big ticket purchases (the down-payment on a newer car, a new refrigerator, new computer equipment, a trip, etc.). Then, once any of that $5,000 is used, replenish as quickly as possible, or you are turning the front wheel on Big Ticket items in the wrong direction.

Guiding principle 4: Set aside college funds. Perhaps you are beginning to wonder where all of the money you need for such a plan will come from. Perhaps you are also beginning to see the importance of Guiding Principle 1: Set a family nurturing income goal. Early planning can make a big difference. Putting off starting college savings until your first senior graduates from high school can prove disastrous. It is important to set aside (absolutely every month) a small fixed amount (or percentage of earnings) to be invested into Certificates of Deposit (CDs) at your bank, or in government securities, or enroll in one of the state college plans for the college cost for each child and NEVER use that money for anything except college costs.

Many states, including Virginia, provide college financing plans that are paid-ahead of the actual need and tuition at good discounts at state colleges (529 plans). The sooner these plans are investigated and purchased, the lower the annual costs. Most families need some type of financial assistance with college funding. Student loans may be appropriate for college juniors and seniors to take out in their own names to pay off later once they are in the full-time work place.

Later, if your students can take over their own costs during their junior or senior years (as I did for my mom and dad) with student loans in the student's names, then you should use any left-over funds in the CDs or other investments for your Retirement Funding (Guiding Principle 5). My parents could not afford my full college cost, and I was glad to help with a student loan. My work during my junior and senior years also immensely helped me prepare for real work. As a college student, I never regretted the student loan. In fact, I learned much about financial responsibility and accountability through that opportunity.

Guiding principle 5: Set aside (begin now) a retirement fund. As another vital allocation of your monthly income, you should set aside (absolutely every month) a fixed amount (or percentage of earnings) into a third account, an Individual Retirement Account (IRA) at your bank, with a stock broker, or a 401(k) plan account through your employer. All money deposited in the conventional IRAs and 401(k)'s (within their limits) are made from pre-tax funds and withdrawals at retirement are subject to income taxes. Also consider Roth IRAs which must be made from after-tax funds, but they grow tax free and withdrawals at retirement are not subject to income taxes. Discuss these and other options with your financial advisors to determine what would be best for you. Always diversify your retirement fund investments. NEVER invest all of your retirement or investment funds with any one person, and NEVER with a friend. Rather than investing in individual stocks and securities, investing in multiple (mutual) funds through a large investment company or companies is an effective approach for many people.

You should NEVER use this retirement money for anything, except retirement after you reach retirement, or you will face stiff penalties. Skipping this guiding principle is like turning the front wheel on your retirement bike in the wrong direction resulting in a huge crash when you retire.

How much do you need to set aside? For example, suppose you determine that you and your spouse as empty nesters can live on $80,000 per year in retirement, considering anticipated inflation between now and retirement, and including taxes and other costs. Suppose too, that social security benefits, plus any company retirement benefits, and plus possible part time income during retirement will take care of about half of the $80,000, leaving the remaining $40,000 as what you need to extract each year from your own set-aside retirement accounts including IRAs, CDs, 401(k) plans and all other fund investments for retirement.

In this example, how much money would you need to have in those retirement funds in order to fund that amount of $40,000 a year for maybe 20 years? Retirement consultants suggest if you keep your annual withdraws from your retirement funds to 4% or less of your total retirement investment portfolio value, you most likely would not run out of money during your lifetime. Using $40,000 and the 4% as an example, that calculates to a total of $1,000,000 required in a retirement portfolio upon retirement. That was figured by dividing the $40,000 by .04 which = $1,000,000. If you think you can live on $20,000 annual withdrawals (instead of the $40,000) the total required would drop to $500,000. That's a still lot of money. The point here is that retirement funding, like college funding, requires early planning and the early building of another mandatory set-aside fund.

Guiding principle 6: Be certain that both spouses have adequate life insurance, legal wills, powers of attorney documents and adequate medical directives. Consider long term care too. At least once a year, have an accountability checkup and review all of your documents and funds' performances and planning with your financial and legal advisors.

Things are a little more complicated now than they were when Dad reviewed his shoe box budget and spending monitoring system with me. But the principles are much the same. Now we have faster tools like computers, the Internet and excellent family finance software available. With these new tools make sure your expenses are fully accountable in real time and budgeted alongside your earnings. Use all Twelve Words in your financial goals and management as systemic guidelines.

Life's Computer Program

The following is a little poem pretending to be a computer program written for people. We might call it an example of people-ware (with apologizes to software). The function of the program is to help us see examples within the program of possible results from certain life-choices along the way.

Sometimes we are like computers -- vain,

running programs buried in our brain,

often from fears, or peers or louder cheers,

or intense work in chosen careers,

maybe burning dry. Loops void of peace,

looking for a chip from other spheres,

a code, in which joy will never cease.

Pause and run this software here.

Follow directions in every line,

learning beyond, a step at a time,

and meet me at your chosen pier.

1 – Consider life's great truths.

2 – Need more stuff?

3 – If yes, go to line 5.

4 – If no, go to line 10.

5 – Buy more stuff.

6 – Count stuff.

7 – Wonder if something is missing?

8 – Consider having more stuff.

9 – Go to line 1.

10 – Consider life's great truths.

11 – Need more fun?

12 – If yes, go to line 14.

13 – If no, go to line 19.

14 – Find more fun.

15 – Enjoy more fun.

16 – Wonder if something is missing?

17 – Consider having more fun.

18 – Go to line 10.

19 – Consider life's great truths.

20 – Need more recognition?

21 – If yes, go to line 23.

22 – If no, go to line 28.

23 – Do something people will admire.

24 – Enjoy the affirmation from others.

25 – Wonder if something is missing?

26 – Consider other credit-worthy options.

27 – Go to line 19.

28 – Realize only 25% of the Universe's mass is visible,
.   even with all of sciences' x-ray instruments.

29 – Ever wonder about the invisible 75%?

30 – If no, go to line 32.

31 – If yes, go to line 37.

32 – Increase your quiet time.

33 – Listen in meditative silence.

34 – Find any clues?

35 – If yes, go to line 37.

36 – If no, go to line 28.

37 – Consider where to shine your light.

38 – Want to share it freely, too?

39 – If yes, go to line 41.

40 – If no, go to line 37.

41 – Consider what you discover in giving.

42 – Listen in meditative silence.

43 – Trust being guided beyond self?

44 – If yes, go to line 46.

45 – If no, go to line 41.

46 – The Divine is here. Celebrate together. Go to line 1.

~ ~ ~

Why ACCOUNTABILITY is Important

I am reminded of my early days of learning to play tennis. Actually learning to play the game is not difficult, is it? The hard part is learning how to hit the ball accurately. My coaches and advisors suggested I spend several hours a day hitting tennis balls against a wall, chasing down the rebound before it bounced twice, and hitting it again, over and over. I was told to work up to a dozen consistent rebound hits. Later, I added a net line on the wall and repeated the pattern again and again. Once I could hit a dozen consistently just above the net line, I was to meet the coach on the tennis court and we would shoot for a dozen there. That's how I learned to accurately hit the ball – after hours and hours of hitting that fuzzy yellow ball against the wall. Once I learned that skill, I thoroughly enjoyed the game for years and years.

Now, let's look at that "wall practicing" as it relates to this subject of accountability. Training eye-hand coordination is a good example of experiencing and benefitting from accountability. When we fail at something (the first hit) the attitude must be, "that wasn't good. I'll try again." If the attitude instead is something like, "stupid ball has a flaw in it... no wonder it missed the wall," then we step out of the classroom of learning and into the busy hallways of protective shielding. The only way to learn skills like this is not to accept a failed attempt as okay. Go to the next level of learning and try again. Accountability.

The idea is not to give up. Don't blame something or someone else. Let the failures be the food that feeds the next try. Failure begs for "M" points. Seize that feedback from each under-achievement action. Remember from the previous chapter, that seizing feedback ("M" points) helps complete the EMA Cycle. Learn to crave "M" points to help you improve in your next try. Then you will be able to visualize that very next step. So try again. That process is true in tennis, in golf, and in life.

See the importance of accountability. In fact, how can one learn anything without accounting for errors made on a previous attempt, and using that to encourage a corrective next try? Truth is, you can't. Accountability is the engine of learning, playing sports, running a business, teaching a class, managing your finances – and it is particularly healthy for children learning how to grow up.

Deep-seated self-confidence comes from many personal experiences with accountability. Fake self-confidence comes from being denied the opportunity to experience failure. Remember the young cashier who could not make change at the beginning of this chapter? Perhaps his inability to work through the process of making change grew from being "protected" from accountability failures by a parent or in school.

Failing to manage your finances at a fully accountable level is like hitting the tennis ball against the wall and then walking away before it bounces back. Why would anyone do that? What could anyone possibly learn by doing that?

Remember – Responsibility is Accountability with a Future.

~ ~ ~

APPENDIX

As noted in the Word Four chapter, God, here is a quote for those interested in further details in the quantum physics experiments mentioned, here from my book, Thin Places and Five Clues in Their Architecture.

What does "science" say about this?

This question intrigues me, because science suggests not only the possibility of thin places (as not capitalized), but also the probability. Quantum physics, the physics of the sub-atomic world, has recently turned a number of conventional Newtonian laws of physics, which we currently live by, on its heels, disproving some of them and seriously questioning others.

For example, the scientific world has generally agreed with Albert Einstein's assertion that the speed of light is the universe's maximum speed limit. Nothing can travel faster. Yet now, quantum physicists have successfully shown that electrons can jump out of their orbits and relocate themselves vast distances away (essentially anywhere in the universe) and they do so instantly. In other words, they are not limited to the speed of light but relocate instantly.

Also, they leave no trace or track of their position in between the two points. They disappear from one place, and reappear instantly million of miles away. Both of these examples are contrary to conventional laws of physics, yet both are happening now. An excellent source of this "new science" information can be found in Leadership and the New Science, Discovering Order in a Chaotic World. Second Edition, by Margaret J. Wheatley, Berrett-Koehler Publications, San Francisco, 1999.

Another recent discovery from quantum physics is particularly relevant here and is also documented in Wheatley's book. Scientists can take paired electrons (similar to twins) and confirm that they are spinning in opposite directions. Then, if the rotating axis of one of the electrons is tilted, the other electron of the pair immediately adjusts its own axis to the same but opposite angle. <u>Scientists have also shown that the distance between the pair has no effect on their ability to maintain a relationship and some form of communication</u>. They can show, for example, that if we separate paired electrons and place one of them in an orbit around Jupiter and then tilt the axis of its spin, the other electron, still here, will instantly tilt its axis the exact same amount in the opposite direction. This astonishing connection is referred to as instantaneous non-local communication.

Now, how might this apply to Thin Places? Scientists know today there are about 23,000,000,000,000,000,000,000,000,000 electrons within each of us, depending on our weight. Consider the unlimited possibilities of communication pathways to and from us and other parts of the universe. Consider how many non-local communication possibilities there might be between worlds.

Based on the thin place evidence gathered and shared over thousands of years, coupled with the relatively recent discoveries in quantum physics, the number of non-local instantaneous communication possibilities before us is well beyond our human capacity to even count them or begin to fully understand.

But in similar ways to how we work with the invisible wind, magnetic fields and electricity, we also work with behaviors and reactions in order to partially understand unseen powers and harness some of the potentials for human good. We have the same opportunities with Thin Places: to learn as much as we can about how and why we are so influenced by certain configurations and links with history. Then, perhaps we can apply reasoning and structuring of Thin Place patterns and invest that knowledge in new environmental practices. That aim is what this book is all about. I begin in Chapter 2 with a recounting of what I experienced during my first Thin Place surprise when I was just 12 years old.

The Boy with the Kite

When I was about 12 years old, I was part of a group of neighborhood guys who gathered on a vacant lot to fly kites. On this particular day, the wind was just right. As we were piloting our kites, a well dressed young boy walked up to me and asked if he could join us. He had what looked like a brand new kite and a ball of clean white string. I had never seen him before. "Sure," I said," need any help?" He nodded yes. I handed my kite string to a friend for a moment. In a few minutes the new boy's kite was up there with the rest of ours. I got my kite string back and kept on flying. I looked over at the new boy, and saw him grinning from ear to ear.

Suddenly though, his kite began to do loop-de-loops. The boy froze, and his kite started looping faster, usually a sign of a crash coming up. But this was worse than a simple crash, because his was headed for the power lines. Several of us yelled, "Move back...pull it back!" Then we all watched it crash onto the top of the power lines. The little boy was horrified. He pulled on the string, but his kite had one of its corners caught under one of the wires, and it wouldn't budge. He dropped his string and turned to me with tears streaming down his face.

"Let me see what I can do," I said, realizing that this was basically hopeless. Then, I wondered if I could walk my kite over to his, pull my kite in some, and maybe nudge his just a bit. More than likely, this could be a two-kite fatality. My kite slowly got closer to his kite. I tried several times to lightly hit his kite, but each time, I would either hit the wires on miss everything. Then in one final attempt, my kite got stuck with his on top of the power lines. My suspicions of a two-kite fatality appeared to be confirmed. I had learned to never pull a tangled kite hard, because that just makes it worse. So, I stood there for a moment, among the silence of sadness, and waited – trying to figure out what to do. Then, a puff of wind blew by – and to my amazement it lifted my kite straight up and above the power lines. And, in the process, even more amazingly, it nudged the boy's kite loose. Cheers went up from all of us as we watched it drift to the ground.

The young boy ran over to the kite, picked it up and ran back to me, carrying his still fresh kite and now even a wider grin. When he got to me, I was ready to tell him, "You're welcome." No big deal. But when he got there, and we were facing each other about 3 feet apart, I saw the look in his eyes. It was powerful and penetrating, and I don't remember him saying any words at all, although I'm sure he did. His eyes revealed a very strong outpouring of gratitude and appreciation that I wasn't prepared for. I think I said, "You're welcome." At least I hope I did. Then the little boy was gone, with his kite. I never saw him again. Maybe he was from out of town visiting an uncle or someone near the vacant lot.

Over the years, I kept seeing that look in his eyes. I believe that's why I never forgot meeting him and his kite. In fact, his eyes haunted me off and on for many years. From time to time in my career as an architect, I would see that same look in someone's eyes I had assisted or helped in some way. Now, many years later, I wonder who was really looking through the boy's eyes out at me and leaving me with an important message. What a powerful delivery system! What a powerful message!

When I was 12 years old, of course I didn't know anything about Thin Places, or much else. I just saw a very strong expression from a person, and for some reason, I sensed I might learn more about this in years to come.

Later I learned that the Cosmic Truth has unlimited ways of reaching us with important messages. The history of Thin Places around the world suggests that such places may be one of the ways. And, now I believe that the small 3 foot space the young boy and I shared, at that very moment, became my first Thin Place experience. Little did I know that about 4 years later I would stumble upon another one.

QUICK ORDER FORMS
For Book and Calendar Ordering,
and FREE Information

--- Now Available ---
TWELVE WORDS full color wall Calendar,
a great way to refer to each of the Twelve Words
and their personal meanings to you each month.

Quick Order Form

To order additional copies of
TWELVE WORDS Never to Forget

Go to: http://stores.lulu.com/pagehighfill

Order Page's calendars and other books at the same website.
Full color Calendar **Twelve Words** Never to Forget

and **Thin Places and Five Clues in Their Architecture**.

To request FREE information, send an e-mail with
your request including the information below to:
Info@EnterPaths.com

Please send **FREE** information on:

☐ Other Books   ☐ Speaking/Programs

☐ Our e-mailing list   ☐ Downloads Available

Name: _____

Address: _____

City: _____ State: _____ Zip:_____

E-mail address: _____

QUICK ORDER FORMS
For Book and Calendar Ordering,
and FREE Information

--- Now Available ---
TWELVE WORDS full color wall Calendar,
a great way to refer to each of the Twelve Words
and their personal meanings to you each month.

Quick Order Form

To order additional copies of
TWELVE WORDS Never to Forget

Go to: http://stores.lulu.com/pagehighfill

Order Page's calendars and other books at the same website.
Full color Calendar **Twelve Words** Never to Forget
and **Thin Places and Five Clues in Their Architecture**.

To request FREE information, send an e-mail with
your request including the information below to:
Info@EnterPaths.com

Please send **FREE** information on:

☐ Other Books ☐ Speaking/Programs

☐ Our e-mailing list ☐ Downloads Available

Name: _____

Address: _____

City: _____ State: _____ Zip:_____

E-mail address: _____

www.ingramcontent.com/pod-product-compliance
Lightning Source LLC
LaVergne TN
LVHW011233080426
835509LV00005B/473